# Alfred Wallis

For my wife and family

# Alfred Wallis
## Artist and Mariner

Robert Jones
foreword by Jovan Nicholson

FIRST LIGHT

First published in Great Britain in 2001
Revised edition 2006
Revised edition 2018
Revised edition 2021

Copyright © 2001, 2006, 2018, 2021 Robert Jones

All rights reserved. No part of this publication may be reproduced, stored in a retrieval system, or transmitted in any form or by any means without the prior permission of the copyright holder.

British Library Cataloguing-in-Publication Data.
A CIP record for this title is available from the British Library.

ISBN 978 1 9996457 2 1

FIRST LIGHT STUDIO Ltd
www.robertjonesartist.com

Also by Robert Jones:
*Alfred Wallis Artist and Mariner* published 2001, revised 2006, revised 2018.
*Reuben Chappell, Pierhead Painter* published 2006.
Catalogue essays:
Tokyo Metropolitan Teien Art Museum, Japan. Major Alfred Wallis retrospective.
Museum Folkwang, Essen, Germany. *The Shadow of the Avant Garde* 2016.
Borlase Smart John Wells Trust, St Ives. Catalogue essays for Sotheby's, Christie's, Bonhams, Lawrences, Roseberys, WH Lane.

Note: Alfred Wallis did not use artists' oil paint. Throughout this book the terms 'oil on card' refers to oil-based household and enamel paints.

*Every effort has been made to track down copyright holders and to obtain their permission for the reproduction of artwork or the quotation of written material. We apologise for any errors or omissions and would be grateful to be informed of any corrections that should be incorporated in future editions of this book.*

*Designed by Allen Greenall*

# Acknowledgements

The author gratefully acknowledges the help of the following individuals:

My wife and amanuensis Susie for her dedication; designer Allen Greenall for his good work and patience; Jovan Nicholson for his ongoing support; David Hawkins; Jenny Pery; Telfer Stokes; Frances Nicholson; Raf Appleby; Shirley Nicholson; Pippa Stilwell; Andy Blair; Bill Wallis; John McWilliams; Andrew Lanyon; Nigel Baker; Pauline Leverett; Dr Tim Rogers.

I would like to thank Andrew Nairne, Dr Jennifer Powell and staff at Kettle's Yard, University of Cambridge; Mr and Mrs Stevens, St Ives Museum; Tony Pawlyn and staff, Bartlett Library, National Maritime Museum, Falmouth; Janet Axten, Graham Smith and volunteers at St Ives Archive; St Ives Times & Echo; Katie Herbert, Penlee House Gallery & Museum, Penzance; Cornwall Record Office; Devon Record Office; Robin Cawdron-Stewart, Sotheby's, London; Ingram Reid, Bonhams; Nigel Strick and Ben Adams, Trading Standards, Cornwall; Memorial University of Newfoundland; Morrab Library, Penzance; Antonia Reeve (photographs on p56, p79 and p108) and Elizabeth Knowles.

I am grateful to the many individuals who allowed me to use images of paintings in their private collections and to all the galleries and archives who provided images and who are individually credited in the text.

# Contents

**FOREWORD** 7
by Jovan Nicholson

**INTRODUCTION** 8

**EARLY LIFE** 14
North Corner, Devonport
The Royal Albert Bridge

**ATLANTIC VOYAGES** 26
Susan Ward
*Pride of the West*
Telegraph
*Belle Aventure*
The Salt Cod Trade
Sailing Vessels
Steamships

**MOUNTS BAY** 58
*Golden Light*
*Alpha & Beta*
Other Voyages

**FALMOUTH** 76
*Nestor*

**FISHING** 90
Cornish Fishing
Pilchard Drivers
Mackerel Drivers
Herring Fishing

**ST IVES** 112
The Marine Stores
Old Iron
An Industrious Man
SS *Rosedale*
Money Matters

**STARTING TO PAINT** 136
St Ives Artist Colony
Starting to Paint
Elizabeth Lewis

**FINDING WALLIS** 144

**A SPRIT OF FREEDOM** 156

**LETTERS** 162

**EVENTS** 170
The Grand Fleet
Airships and Aeroplanes
The Wreck of *Cicelia*
The Wreck of SS *Alba*
The Wreck of the lifeboat *John and Sarah Eliza Stych*
Steamer in a Rough Sea
The Wreck of SS *Bluejacket*
Visiting Boats, East Coast Boats and Newlyn Riots
Brixham Sailing Trawlers
French Fishing Boats

**WALLIS'S VISION** 200
Maps of the Sea
St Ives Bay Paintings
The Seine Fishery

**THE LAST YEARS** 216
Madron
Sketchbooks

**APPENDIX I** 230
Our Views of Wallis
Never at sea
Bill Wallis
Forgeries

**APPENDIX II** 242
Recorded Memories
People who knew Alfred Wallis
Dr Roger Slack's recorded memories of Alfred Wallis

Endnotes 256

*St Ives Harbour, low tide; 19th century*
Photo: St Ives Archive

# Foreword

Alfred Wallis's paintings stand on their own as wonderful evocations of life at sea with all the dramas that involved. But when we know the details and facts behind Wallis's works this gives them a further and deeper meaning. This is the world that Robert Jones has opened up for us. To be able to read the ships registers and to see proof that Wallis crossed the Atlantic Ocean in the schooner *Pride of the West* and returned in *Belle Aventure* gives us a greater understanding of the drama Wallis lived through and what he meant to convey in his paintings of those boats. It explains why he depicted a schooner riding a steep wave of the North Atlantic swell, or the icebergs he witnessed off Newfoundland and it elucidates the significance of the paintings of the wonderfully named mackerel lugger he served in, The *Flying Scud PZ11*. We know from Ben Nicholson that Alfred Wallis 'enjoyed talking about his paintings, speaking about them not as paintings but as actual experiences'. The knowledge that Robert Jones has unlocked allows us to imagine how Wallis talked about and described his paintings to his friends. And this draws us much closer to his creativity.

The information Robert Jones has painstakingly gathered is more extensive than just about the boats Wallis sailed in, but includes fascinating details about the locations he knew intimately with their buoys, rocks and channels, which Wallis so accurately recorded in his chart-like paintings of Mount's Bay and St Ives Bay. Who but a mariner who knew the sea in Mount's Bay would depict the Gear Pole so precisely? Or the buoy marking the sand bar at the entrance to the channel at Hayle?

A Cornish painter with maritime experience, Robert Jones also dispels many of the myths and falsities that have sprung up about Alfred Wallis and his life, in particular the somewhat irritating fallacy that he never went to sea. Thankfully, because of Robert's meticulous research, we can now dismiss this absurd idea, and freely muse on how Wallis's intimate knowledge and experience of the sea inform his paintings.

When so little was previously known about Alfred Wallis, both his life and creativity, Robert Jones's book is essential reading for anyone who cares deeply about this highly original artist who led such a fascinating and tragic life. This book about Alfred Wallis is a testament to Robert Jones's dedication and persistence. It is a singular achievement.

*Jovan Nicholson, 2018*

# Introduction

Alfred Wallis started painting in 1925 at the age of seventy. He said that it was 'for company', after the death of his wife. From memory, he painted the experiences of his early life - his sea voyages, ships he had seen, the harbours he visited and the town of St Ives as he knew it. Wallis had an extraordinary visual memory. Many of his pictures are rich in nautical, historical and geographical detail, and contain a wealth of knowledge about a way of life that has gone forever. Wallis himself was aware of this, and

> *would talk of his paintings as if they were old photographs, instructive documents designed to inform a younger generation of what the world was like in the old days* [1]

He was painting his memories of scenes that had disappeared and he often referred in his letters to

> *'mosley what use To Bee'* and *'what we may never see again'.* [2]

His paintings do indeed tell of a way of life and a rich culture that has passed. Throughout this book the paintings Wallis made from his memories in his latter years illustrate the story of his life.

From his childhood in the small harbour town of North Corner on the banks of the Tamar, we learn that he went to sea at an early age and spent years working on sailing ships as a seaman. Ships' records reveal a voyage across the Atlantic from Penzance a few weeks after his marriage to Susan Ward in 1876.

While he was working as a seaman and later as a fisherman with the Newlyn and Mousehole fleets Wallis and his wife lived in Penzance, as did his brother Charles who ran a marine scrap business. In the mid 1880s the couple moved to St Ives to run a similar business. The Marine Stores business lasted over 30 years and Wallis's call as he toured the town with his donkey and cart earned him the nickname 'old iron'.

During those years a growing number of artists had come to settle and work in St Ives, attracted by the unique quality of reflected light that comes from the sea and sand surrounding the peninsula. The arrival of the Great Western Railway in 1877 made the area more accessible and a significant art colony was formed in the lively harbour town. The seascapes and landscapes these artists produced were predominantly topographical, and based on observation. Painters were concerned with light and atmosphere and were often to be seen working outside, *en plein air*. The presence of so many artists in St Ives may have affected Wallis's decision to take up painting but, remarkably, their work seems to have had little or no influence on him. His art came from a different source: his memory and his own experiences. Thus, his work informs us of facts and events, and has more in common with medieval art, early Renaissance painters and the art of ancient civilisations.

Using discarded materials, he made paintings with household and enamel paint and pencil on bits of cardboard or wood. The work of this untrained artist who had scant understanding of perspective meant very little to the artists in the town who considered accuracy of scale and perspective integral to their craft.

### The Island, St Ives

Oil and pencil on card, 9¼ x 10¾ in (23.3 x 27.5 cm) Whitworth Art Gallery, Manchester

*This painting shows us the buildings on The Island at St Ives, St Nicholas Chapel and the Coastguard building with its signal mast used for storm warnings and generally signalling to ships.*

Wallis's pictures were no more valued by his friends and neighbours; many of the paintings given to them by Wallis were thrown away or burnt, as ruefully testified by people who had known Wallis.

Ben Nicholson and Christopher Wood were on a day visit to St Ives in 1928 when they discovered Wallis. They recognised something fresh in his childlike, naive paintings and they valued Wallis's simple, direct and honest approach. His paintings represented a freedom of expression to which they themselves aspired. Through them, Wallis's work was introduced to a small circle of artists and collectors, whose interest and encouragement inspired him. Without this support, we might speculate that the value of Wallis's art would have been unrecognised and his paintings simply chucked away and forgotten. It transpired that the artists who appreciated Wallis would become leading figures in the British Modernist movement. His art profoundly affected their work, and through his influence there is a direct link from Wallis to the abstract art of the Modernist period that was to follow.

For the last fifteen years of his life, Wallis's output was prolific. He is now regarded as one of the most unique and original artists of the twentieth century.

Wallis made his paintings on his kitchen table in the front room of his cottage in Back Road West, St Ives. As a seaman he would have been familiar with nautical charts; when painting the harbours of Mount's Bay and St Ives Bay he looked down on his paintings and had an innate ability to visualise sea and land as if from the air. His paintings depict features of significance to the mariner and can be read as maps of the sea.

An intensely religious man, Wallis would neither paint nor sell paintings on Sundays as he believed that money should not change hands on the Sabbath. On Sunday he would cover his paintings with newspaper and read the Bible.

I come to Wallis from a unique point of view. I grew up on the north coast of Cornwall; the cliffs and beaches around Newquay and the harbour were the playground of my childhood and youth. For me, Wallis's paintings embody something of the wildness of the Cornish coast I know so well.

I have drawn and painted all my life and was a student at Falmouth School of Art in the 1960s. There I saw some small, black and white reproductions of Wallis's paintings in an art magazine. A nearby article on American Expressionism discussed the work of Willem de Kooning and Franz Kline, again illustrated in black and white. It struck me that when reduced to similar sizes, Wallis's pictures had much of the grit and presence that made the American artists' work so powerful.

In 1968 I visited the Arts Council exhibition of Alfred Wallis's work at the Penwith Gallery, St Ives. The exhibition was curated by Sir Alan Bowness, and it continued to the Tate Gallery in London and toured other galleries around the country. Around the same time I read the original 1967 version of Edwin Mullins's book *Alfred Wallis: Cornish Primitive Painter*, a wonderful introduction to Wallis's work.

My own experience of the sea has also informed my interpretation of Wallis's paintings. In the 1970s I spent seven years as skipper of various fishing boats working the inshore waters around the coast of Cornwall. In summer we fished from Hayle and St Ives Bay for lobsters and crabs, and in winter we worked from Newlyn and Falmouth fishing the large shoals of mackerel that were abundant at that time.

We were fishing the very places that appear in many of Wallis's paintings and I began to notice features and details in his paintings that left me in no doubt that his work was made from his real experiences. For example, many of Wallis's depictions of St Ives Bay feature the buoy that marks the channel and the entrance to Hayle harbour. Known as the Bar Buoy and hardly noticeable to the layman, this is an essential marker for vessels entering and leaving Hayle; a passage which can, at times, be treacherous. The more I looked at Wallis's paintings, the more I recognised such details. I became increasingly fascinated by the process of identifying the sources of imagery in his work. I grew interested in the history of Cornish fishing and particularly the merchant shipping of Wallis's time, which led me to settle once and for all the question of whether or not Wallis actually went to sea.

A distant relative from Wallis's adopted family, Albert Rowe, wrote a book called *Boy and the Painter: Scenes from Alfred Wallis's Life* (published in 1957) about growing up in St Ives and his early recollections of Wallis, including a remark from his grandfather who dismissed Alfred Wallis's seagoing stories as fantasies because 'he wasn't exactly right in the head' and 'Alfred had never been to sea in his life.' The implication that Wallis was a fantasist was thus given publicity and credibility and influenced critics such as David Sylvester.[3] The issue was discussed by Mullins in *Cornish Primitive Painter*.

To my mind, there can be no doubt that Wallis went to sea. The visual evidence is in his paintings, his clear knowledge of vessels, coast and harbours speaks for itself. However, Peter Barnes has done a great deal of research into the Wallis family history and has found Alfred Wallis's name on the crew agreement of a ship that sailed from St John's, Newfoundland to Teignmouth. Subsequently, I found his signature on a crew agreement of a ship that took him on the first part of that voyage, from Penzance to Cadiz and then to Newfoundland. These crew agreements provide indisputable evidence of the voyages he made in 1876 to Newfoundland and back, in connection with the salt cod trade.

**PZ 364 Michael and David** by Susan Jones 1978
Oil on board

*"In summer we worked out of the port of Hayle on the north Cornish coast; each day we crossed St Ives Bay on our way to the fishing grounds where we worked 450 pots to catch crab and lobster.*
*In autumn we took the boat around Lands End, spending the winter in Newlyn or Falmouth following the huge shoals of mackerel that came to the south coast of Cornwall in those days". (Robert Jones)*

The doubts sown by Albert Rowe have affected the way Wallis has been portrayed over the years. We have been given a distorted view of the seaman and artist, which I hope this book will dispel. I was privileged to know Dr Roger Slack, who came to St Ives as a GP in 1947. Although Wallis had died by the time Dr Slack arrived, he made tape recorded interviews with local people who knew the artist. This material gives a very illuminating picture of Wallis as seen by the people around him.

*Alfred Wallis: Artist and Mariner* was first published in 2001, with a second edition in 2006. In 2007 an exhibition of Wallis's work was held at the Tokyo Metropolitan Teien Art Museum. I wrote an essay about the sources of Wallis's imagery for the catalogue and was invited to give an illustrated talk at the Museum. I have also given talks in art galleries and universities in Britain, including at Kettle's Yard, University of Cambridge where the largest and most important collection of Wallis's work is housed, created by Jim Ede in the 1930s. Auction houses and individuals sometimes ask for my advice on Wallis and I have assisted Trading Standards in successfully carrying through two significant fraud cases involving Alfred Wallis fakes. I have included a description of these events in this edition (see page 228).

Over recent years more information has emerged, and this has opened up new avenues of research. I have spoken to people about their childhood memories of Wallis. Rewriting certain passages has allowed me to clarify my thoughts. To understand this artist, it is important to grasp that his paintings originated from his personal life experience. If these pictures were works of the imagination they would still be wonderful paintings but we would see them in an entirely different light. Throughout this study, I particularly draw attention to the wealth of visual information contained in the paintings themselves and hope that this approach will aid the understanding and appreciation of Wallis's unique art.

**Headland with Two Three-masters**
Oil on card, 11⅝ x 10¾ in (23.3 x 27.5 cm) Pier Arts Centre, Orkney

# Early Life
## North Corner Devonport

*19th century postcard.
Boats and waterfront buildings, North Corner, Devonport.*

The River Tamar separates the counties of Devon and Cornwall. On its eastern bank lies the historic naval town of Devonport. A waterside area of the town known as North Corner is squeezed between two large naval dockyards where great warships were built and repaired. Alfred Wallis was born at 5 Pond Lane, North Corner, Devonport. The date on his birth certificate is 8th August 1855. Devonport was a colourful place then, with plenty of public houses to cater for the needs and vices of sailors, seamen and dockworkers; at times the area could be rough and lawless.

Peter Barnes's research into Wallis's early life and family background shows that his parents, Charles and Jane Wallis, originally came from Cornwall. They were married in Penzance in 1844. Charles's occupation at that time was recorded as 'sailor'.

*Charles consistently gave Penzance, Cornwall as his place of birth. His wife Jane gave Penzance as her place of birth in the 1851 Census and the Isles of Scilly as her birth place in the 1861 Census. Whichever it was she would have been regarded as Cornish. Since Alfred chose to live in Cornwall all his adult life it could be said that by blood and inclination he was a Cornishman who had the misfortune of being born a few hundred yards on the wrong side of the Tamar.* [4]

Alfred's older brother Charles was named after his father and there was at least one other child, Mary, who died in infancy. Barnes suggests that since Charles and Jane Wallis were married for twenty-two years, it is likely that there were other children. However, only Charles and Alfred survived.

The Wallis family had been living in a succession of rented properties in the North Corner area since 1851. Their presence there was undoubtedly due to the fact that Charles senior had employment in the area. On various census forms and the birth certificates of his children he was recorded as a 'pavior' (one who lays paving stones) and a 'hammer man in a coach factory'.

Although it is likely that Wallis grew up in what today would be regarded as poverty, he did have some schooling. The 1861 census described six year old Alfred as 'a scholar', the term used for 'schoolboy'. At that time the Wallis family were living near Cornwall Street where, in 1860, St Paul's Parochial School was built. The building was demolished in 2000 and unfortunately school records only exist from 1895 onwards. However, Wallis's letters written in later life show a controlled, copper-plate script, typical of the handwriting style that was taught in those days.

The streets of North Corner run downhill to the quay and jetty, where this busy stretch of the Tamar, known as the Hamoaze, flows past the Royal Naval Dockyard and North Corner to the sea. Large naval vessels regularly passed by, and a great variety of ships called at the quay. The familiar sight of naval ships, ferries, river steamers and merchant ships carrying passengers and goods must have left a lasting impression on the young Alfred Wallis.

*19th century postcard.*
*The harbour and jetty, North Corner, Devonport.*

*Above:* HMS Aurora

*Below:* HMS Hood

*19th century postcard. The jetty at North Corner with Royal Naval Battleship* Hood *1891.*
*The quays and waterfront of North Corner undoubtedly provided a fascinating playground for Wallis at a formative time in his life.*

**Gunboat in War Time**

Oil on panel, 7¼ x 12¼ in (18.5 x 31.1 cm) Private Collection

*This painting of warships passing a jetty is perhaps a memory of the Hamoaze, witnessed by Wallis during his childhood in North Corner, Devonport. In the second half of the nineteenth century, the backward-sloping bows and prominent crow's nest lookouts were a feature of Royal Naval warships. These vessels were known as 'ironclads' and the later dreadnoughts had similar features.*

*Construction of the Royal Albert Bridge 1858.*
Photo: Private Collection
*Two Westcountry schooners are shown in the photograph. In those days, such ships were commonplace.*

## The Royal Albert Bridge

A photograph taken from the banks of the River Tamar shows the construction of Isambard Kingdom Brunel's extraordinary engineering achievement, the Royal Albert Bridge, which spanned the river just two miles north of Wallis's childhood home. The bridge opened in 1859 and took the Great Western Railway from Devon and the rest of Britain, into Cornwall. It reached Penzance in 1876 and St Ives in 1878. The bridge must have been a spectacular sight, and the arrival of the railway brought huge social and economic change. This new structure clearly left a lasting impression: over sixty years later, Wallis was to tap his memory, depicting the bridge and its environs in his paintings many times.

*Aerial view of the River Tamar showing the Royal Albert Bridge.*
Photo: Private Collection
*Devonport and North Corner on the shore to the left, and the sea beyond.*

*Royal Albert Bridge, c.1889.*
Photo: Private Collection

Old sailing ships, the 'men-of-war' of a past era, were moored on the Hamoaze and in Wallis's time they were used to train teenage boys who were to become recruits in the Royal Navy. On such vessels, the lads were equipped with the skills and discipline necessary for naval life. *HMS Implacable* and *HMS Impregnable* were examples of such ships, and Wallis recalled the sight in the painting *Boats Before A Great Bridge*. His memories of the bridge and a viaduct he must have observed elsewhere seem to have been combined in some of his works, as details in the bridge vary.

**Boats Before a Great Bridge**
Oil on panel, 14½ x 15½ in (36.7 x 39.2 cm) Kettle's Yard, University of Cambridge

*Above: HMS* Implacable *was originally a French ship of 74 guns that had fought at Trafalgar and was later captured by the British. She was moored on the Hamoaze, becoming a training ship in 1855.*

*Below: HMS* Impregnable *was a British ship of 98 guns, launched in 1810. She fought in the Battle of Tangiers and saw service in other Mediterranean conflicts. From 1862 she was also moored on the Hamoaze and used as a training ship.*

**Boats Under Saltash Bridge**
Oil on card, 11½ × 19¾ in (30 × 50 cm)
Kettle's Yard, University of Cambridge

Right: **Saltash Bridge**
Pencil and oil on board, 17½ × 23¾ in (44.5 × 60.3 cm)
Image courtesy of Christie's
*A variety of sail and steam vessels lie at anchor in the Hamoaze near the Royal Albert Bridge.*

Far right: **Saltash Bridge**
Pencil and oil on card, 12 × 16¾ in (30.5 × 42.5 cm)
Image courtesy of Bonham's
*A train passes over the Royal Albert Bridge, while below steamships lie at anchor and a sailing boat makes its way under the bridge.*

**Sailing Ship** 1933-1942

Oil on cardboard, 8¾ x 12½ in (22.2 x 31.7 cm) The Lucy Carrington Wertheim Bequest. Towner Art Gallery, Eastbourne

*Painted on the back of an old calendar 1933, a large ship, a barque, sails past the stern of a much larger vessel, which looks like one of the old 'men-of-war' used as training ships and moored on the Hamoaze during Wallis's childhood days in Devonport.*

*Photo of Plymouth Breakwater. Constructed in 1812 at the mouth of the Tamar, the 1,710 yard breakwater protects Plymouth Sound and the anchorages in the waters of the Hamoaze beyond.*

**Three Lighthouses**

Oil on card, 6½ x 12½ in (16.5 x 31.5 cm) Private Collection

*The horizontal feature at the bottom of this painting, which appears upside down to the viewer, represents Plymouth Breakwater. Wallis has depicted this unique geographical feature in other paintings. The breakwater is distinguished by a light at each end, as he has shown.*

Sven Berlin, a painter and sculptor working in St Ives, started researching Wallis's life and work in 1941 before he joined the Army to serve in the Second World War. His first book on Wallis, entitled *Alfred Wallis, Primitive*, was published in 1949.

Berlin did not meet Alfred Wallis. By the time Berlin started to write, Wallis was in Madron Public Assistance Institute. His book was based on conversations with people who had known Wallis, his relatives and neighbours in St Ives and the small circle of artists who collected his work and had visited him. The information Berlin gathered in this way clearly originated from Wallis himself. It provides significant insights into his life, including details of places he had visited and names of ships he had worked aboard. Berlin's accounts of incidents in Wallis's life give us an intriguing view of the artist's character.

It seems reasonable to accept that Wallis first went to sea at an early age. Berlin writes that Wallis was nine years old when he made his first trip across the Bay of Biscay in a schooner. He goes on to state that Wallis spent the next sixteen years as an ordinary seaman working aboard a number of different sailing

**Two Steamers and Lighthouses and Estuary**
Oil on card, laid on board, 10½ x 15½ in (27.5 x 39.5 cm)
Private Collection

*In this painting Wallis shows the two lighthouses and the breakwater to the left of the painting. On the top right an unusual vessel is anchored, this would appear to be a lightship. Wallis remembered the 'ball-cage' daymark at the top of the mast.*

*Lightships were painted bright red and the 'ball-cage' on the mast-head was a distinguishing daymark carried by most early lightships. The lantern was lowered down the mast during the day and brought down to the deck to be serviced and to ease the rolling motion of the vessels.*

vessels. Although we have no documentary evidence to substantiate this, it was not unusual for young boys to go to sea in those days, and at that time there were plenty of opportunities to join one of the many merchant sailing ships on the Tamar.

> *For some years Alfred Wallis worked on the schooners as cabin boy and cook. He was efficient at his job. Indeed, he proved himself capable in everything he set himself to do, both at sea and on land. In spite of his short stature he was wiry and strong. Even in his last years he still retained the nimbleness, speed and surety of balance obtained from his life on the schooners. One must remember how hard that life was, what powers of endurance were needed by the seamen of that time; walking the decks, handling the canvas and rigging of a light 'fore and aft' schooner in a heavy North Atlantic gale called for high physical awareness and courage. Wallis, of course, was an ordinary seaman when he grew older.* [5]

# Atlantic Voyages

In 1866, Alfred Wallis was ten years old when his mother Jane died of tuberculosis. Some time after her death, Charles and his two sons moved from Devonport to Penzance. The 1871 census shows that Charles Wallis was living at 23 Camberwell Street in Penzance with his son Alfred, while his other son, Charles, was living at another address in Penzance.

In the mid-nineteenth century, Penzance was a thriving sea port. In addition to the local fishing fleet and Penzance-registered merchant ships, the harbour was visited by sail and steamships that voyaged around Britain, and to European ports, the Mediterranean and across the Atlantic.

## Susan Ward

While living in Penzance, Wallis came to know Susan Ward through his friendship with her son George. Susan, a widow twenty-one years Wallis's senior, was originally from south Devon. She had come to west Cornwall with her first husband, Jacob to work on the Bolitho Estate situated on the hills above Penzance, overlooking Mount's Bay and near the village of Madron where they lived. When Jacob died in 1872, Susan moved to Penzance with her five children, George, Albert, Emily, Jessie and Jacob.

Wallis moved in with Susan Ward, and when they were married in St Mary's Church on 2nd April 1876 Susan was expecting his child. The address recorded by the registrar was 15 New Street, Penzance, and Wallis's occupation was registered as 'sailor'.

*The house in New Street, Penzance where Alfred Wallis and Susan Ward lived before they were married. Note the similarity between this house and the one on the bottom left of the painting on page 136.*

*Penzance harbour mid-nineteenth century.*
Photo: St Ives Archive

*South Quay, Penzance Harbour photographed in the mid 1870s.*
Photo: Reg Watkiss Collection
*This photograph, taken before the railway reached Penzance in the 1880s, illustrates the importance of shipping at that time. It well evokes the atmosphere of this busy port in the days of sail. In the background are St Mary's Church and the quayside buildings, which look much the same today.*

*Schooner* Pride of the West, *photographed off Penzance.*

Photo: St Ives Archive

Pride of the West *was registered in Penzance in 1875. The ship was less than a year old and was owned by John Matthews of Regent's Terrace, Penzance. The master of the ship was R. Rodd of Penzance. The following is from Lloyds register 1881: ON67015. Registered tonnage 112 gross 99 net. Built by Thomas Massey of Portreath. Launched in July 1875. 87.5 foot x 28.8 x 10.4.*

**Pride of the West**

In spring 1876, a westcountry topsail schooner, *Pride of the West*, was moored alongside the quay in Penzance Harbour. The vessel had arrived there having sailed from Cardiff with a cargo of coal on the 18th March. There had been a minor collision when leaving Cardiff.

*18th March 1876* Pride of the West *left Cardiff lost her jib boom and damaged her sail in a heavy squall. The lights of another schooner were sighted and she tried to keep astern of her, but hampered by loss of sail collided with her, but was unharmed. She reached Penzance on Monday evening.* (Cornish Telegraph)

*21st March 1876* Pride of the West *now discharging her cargo of household and parlour coals at 20/- and 22/- per ton for J P Sampson of 21 Penwith Street.* (Cornish Telegraph)

Less than a year old, the ship was owned by John Matthews of Regent Terrace, Penzance. While in Penzance, the ship would have been refitted and provisioned in preparation for the next voyage. The master, William

Robert Rodd, thirty-four, of Penzance and Scottish cook John MacLennan, sixteen, had stayed with the vessel but the rest of the crew had left the ship, so the owner and master needed to hire experienced seamen.

On 24th April 1876, three men signed articles when joining the ship's crew. They were: Anthony Benson, thirty two, from Penzance, who came aboard as boatswain (second in command), Richard Dusting, twenty-two, also of Penzance, and James Thompson, twenty-one, of Westport, Ireland who had previously been working aboard another Penzance vessel.

On 25th April, three weeks after he and Susan were married, Wallis, then nineteen, joined the ship as an ordinary seaman. *Pride of the West* was to sail from Penzance to St John's, Newfoundland via Cadiz, Spain.

Neither the owner John Matthews nor Master William Rodd would have allowed crewmen to join the ship if they were not competent and experienced seamen. Wallis clearly knew the ropes and understood that the intended voyage was a considerable undertaking; demanding, of both ship and men.

**The Pride of the West** (inscribed with title)
Oil on card 20 x 16 in (50.8 x 40.6 cm) Crane Kalman Gallery, London
*In his seagoing days, Wallis was laying down memories that were the foundations of the paintings he was to make more than fifty years later.*

Pride of the West *Agreement and Account of Crew.*

*Pride of the West*'s Articles of Agreement

On joining *Pride of the West*, Wallis signed an agreement and account of crew. Members of the crew are required to sign such agreements when they join and leave a vessel. These documents record the name and official number of the ship and the names of the owners and the port of registry. The names and ages of the crew, their place of birth and the last ship they served on are also noted. The conditions of service are laid out, including the disciplinary practices and a clarification of what is expected of the crew. The document also states how much money the seamen are to receive for their labours, a description of the possible voyage and the agreed period of employment. A list of the food they will be given may also be present, at times abbreviated to: 'Sufficient No Waste', 'At Master's Option' and 'No Grog Allowed'.

On arrival in a foreign port, ship's articles were deposited with the consulate or shipping office, to be returned when the ship was about to depart. Changes to the crew, the reasons for leaving the ship, monies they received, disputes and so on, were all recorded by the consul or shipping officer. Therefore, articles of agreement give us an accurate picture of how long a vessel stayed in a port and the duration of voyages but do not tell us what cargo a ship was carrying. Sometimes it is possible to make an informed guess, and this is the case here with *Pride of the West*.

During the latter part of the nineteenth century, European ships sailing across the Atlantic to Newfoundland would often call at Cadiz for a cargo of salt, which had long been produced in that area. The salt was used in the Canadian fisheries as a preservative for cod. These vessels, which may also have carried general cargo such as dried fruit or wine, would continue the journey to Newfoundland to collect a cargo of salt cod.

On 26th April 1876, *Pride of the West* left Penzance, sailing down the Western Approaches past Finistère, Brittany and across the Bay of Biscay for Cadiz, arriving on 8th May - a voyage of twelve days. On 12th May, after four days in Cadiz, *Pride of the West* sailed for St John's, Newfoundland, arriving on 10 June, having crossed the Atlantic in just under a month. This was a very reasonable time for a crossing - it being a voyage that could take three months in poor weather.

On 24th June, after two weeks in St John's, time enough to unload the cargo that had been carried from Cadiz, *Pride of the West* set sail again. On 7th July, the ship arrived at Little Glace Bay, Cape Breton Island, Nova Scotia.

Catching, salting and drying cod were not activities exclusive to Newfoundland; there were many cod fishing settlements along the eastern coast of Canada. St John's was the centre of this trade, but it was a competitive business and ships sought cargoes at smaller harbours in Newfoundland, Labrador and Nova Scotia.

While docked in Little Glace Bay, two members of the crew left the ship. No reason is given in the articles, but the shipping officer there recorded that on 7th July Anthony Benson and Alfred Wallis had left the crew and were being 'shipped for passage' back to St John's. They were aboard *Pride of the West* when it departed from Little Glace Bay on 11th July and arrived at St John's on 13th July, where the consul recorded:

*St. John's Newfoundland, August 9. 76 this is to certify that Anthony Benson and Alfred Wallis have been duly discharged in this port by mutual consent and the balance of their wages distributed to them in my presence.* **6**

Written in a heavy hand, it was recorded that Wallis was 'in debt', presumably the charge for his passage from Little Glace Bay to St. John's. *Pride of the West* also carried crew members from a another vessel back to St John's.

We can only speculate as to why Benson and Wallis left the ship. Could there have been problems with the Captain? Were conditions aboard harsh? Was the food bad, the seaworthiness of the ship in question? If this were the case, why did they not leave earlier, when they first reached St John's? It could be that while in Nova Scotia, Captain Rodd had been informed by telegraph that *Pride of the West* was not to return to a British or North European port but was to sail, instead, to the Mediterranean. Was it the case that the two Penzance men were reluctant to face another protracted voyage before returning home?

The articles of agreement do indeed show that *Pride of the West*'s next port of call was Genoa in Italy. It was not unusual for a ship to be ordered to sail to the Mediterranean in this way, as there was a ready market for salt cod in that region and many ships sailed this triangular route before returning to Britain. *Pride of the West* returned to Britain in the spring of 1877.

**Telegraph**

From the mid-1840s, telegraph companies developed a network of cables to be laid alongside the railway system. Messages were transmitted by Morse Code, a series of electronic dots and dashes, which could be sent at the rate of about eight words per minute. Although it was possible at that time to send messages through a commercial network of cables within Britain, Europe and the USA, prior to 1866 there were no transatlantic cables, so ships away on long-haul, deep-sea trades were completely out of contact with their owners and agents. Then, in 1866, *SS Great Eastern* laid the first successful transatlantic cable, linking Ireland to Newfoundland. So in 1876 it was possible for Captain Rodd in Nova Scotia to be in touch with John Matthews, *Pride of the West*'s owner in Penzance.

Pride of the West *Articles of Agreement 1876.*

Wallis's signature appears twice in the ship's articles of agreement on leaving *Pride of the West*. Once, when he and Anthony Benson quit in Little Glace Bay, and again, after being shipped back to St John's, where it is stated that he is 'in debt', presumably for the cost of the passage.

*Belle Aventure*

Having left *Pride of the West*, the two Penzance men, Wallis and Benson, found themselves in St John's, a foreign port a long way from home. We do not know what happened to Benson, but Wallis secured a berth aboard a Devon ship, *Belle Aventure*. He seems to have been very lucky, for two men from that vessel had deserted, and experienced crew were required for the voyage back across the Atlantic. Wallis joined the crew and the ship left St John's bound for Britain on 7th August.

**Belle Aventure of Brixham** (inscribed with title)
Private Collection

Belle Aventure *was registered in Dartmouth. ON 29526, 98 tons net. Owned by N Barker of Brixham, built by Master Edwin Snell of Brixham. The crew agreement on the following page shows that* Belle Aventure *arrived in Seville 24th May 1876 and left on 1st June for Newfoundland, arriving at St John's 14th July, a transatlantic voyage of six weeks. The ship was in St John's for three weeks, time to unload cargo and to load a new one of dry salt cod. Two crewmen deserted* Belle Aventure *in St John's.*

Belle Aventure *Agreement and Account of Crew.*

*... and the spirit of God moved upon the face of the waters. (Genesis 1:2)*

Berlin recounts a story that Wallis told in his later years, in which he described waving farewell to the crew of another ship that left St John's on the 6th August 1876. They departed on a fine day but ran into a heavy gale off the coast and the ship was lost with all hands. The next day, with Wallis aboard, *Belle Aventure* set sail across the Atlantic and also ran into a severe storm. Berlin continues:

*The men fought to the last ounce of energy and endurance, only saving themselves by making a chain and passing the cargo of dead fish up from the hold and throwing it into the sea, allowing the ship to right herself.* [7]

This story has more than a ring of truth about it. In heavy seas, even today, a cargo shifting in a gale can cause a ship to list and become unstable and therefore unsailable. August is the beginning of the season when hurricanes sweep up the east coast of America and Canada. Even when the winds have subsided, huge swells last for days following a hurricane. Any seaman out in these conditions would find this a powerful and awe-inspiring experience.

*Once I saw one of those ocean-going schooners showing what she could do in a howling North-Atlantic gale, with the sea running mountains high as the phrase goes. The sailing ship I was in was under very reduced canvas. As the schooner crossed our bows we could see her leaning over until her lee gunwale was under water. Her three little scraps of sail, not much bigger than handkerchiefs, tore her along at a great pace amid a smother of foam, and clouds of heavy spray and sometimes green water swept her from end to end. We could see two oilskin clad figures at the wheel, they must have been lashed there or they would have been washed away. She seemed a living, mad thing as she rushed down the slope of one wave and up the next.* [8]

**A West Country Schooner on a Swell**
Oil and pencil on card 7½ x 11⅝ in (19 x 29.5 cm) Image courtesy of Lawrences

**Belle Aventure of Brixham** (inscribed with title)
Private Collection

The voyage across the Atlantic took three months. This must have been a difficult journey; perhaps the ship was damaged in the storm. From the crew agreement we learn that *Belle Aventure* arrived in Teignmouth on 4th November 1876. Having been paid £6.12s.4d, Wallis was discharged on 9th November.

It is unlikely that Wallis had received any news from home until he returned from his voyage, only to learn that while he was away the child that Susan had been carrying had been born on 5th July 1876 but had died. The baby was registered as Alfred Charles Wallis, and Wallis's occupation was recorded as 'Mariner, Merchant Service'.

Not long after Wallis returned from Newfoundland, on 9th December 1876, his brother Charles got married. His occupation was recorded in Penzance as 'Marine Store Dealer'. Alfred and Susan witnessed the marriage.

The Wallises continued to live in Penzance. Susan bore another child on 25th May 1879, a girl named Ellen Jane, but she, too, died in infancy. By this time, Wallis was recorded as 'labourer'. Both infants were buried in Madron Cemetery; no stone marks either grave.

The 1881 census states that Charles Wallis and his wife Elizabeth lived with their three children at 3 Gas Street, Penzance. Their youngest child, a son, died shortly after this.

**Schooner and icebergs**
Oil on card 11¼ x 15¾ in (28.6 x 40 cm) Image courtesy Sotheby's

*They that go down to the sea in ships, that do business in great waters; These see the works of the Lord, and his wonders in the deep. For he commandeth, and raiseth the stormy wind, which lifteth up the waves thereof. They mount up to the heavens, they go down again to the depths: (Psalm 107)*

**Schooner Under the Moon**

Oil on card 11½ x 11½ in (29.2 x 29.2 cm) Tate London, 2001

*At night, a schooner climbs a huge Atlantic swell. Such conditions, also known as 'ground sea', can last for days after a storm. Great waves, like hills and valleys, come one after the other and travel across the Atlantic, eventually breaking on western shores.*

**Belle Aventure of Brixham Larbordoor Newfoundland Ice Burges** (inscribed with title on reverse)
Oil and pencil on card 10¾ x 15 in (27.3 x 38.1 cm) Private Collection

*The back of this painting is inscribed by Wallis: 'Belle Aventure of Brixham Larbordoor Newfoundland Ice Burges'. The artist depicts his voyage on* Belle Aventure *as it sails past icebergs. But what a curious, seemingly incongruous, combination. At the top of the painting there are surely trees in blossom. Can this be right? Trees in blossom and icebergs? In fact, this is just what happens in what is known as 'Iceberg Alley'. In spring and summer along the coast of Newfoundland, icebergs that have broken away from the polar icecaps drift south, break up and are washed ashore just as Wallis remembers so vividly.*

**Schooner With Icebergs**

Oil on card 13 x 27¼ in (33 x 69 cm) Private Collection

*What drama this painting evokes! Sailing at night through a sea of icebergs clearly provided a lasting memory for Alfred Wallis.*

*The depiction of the moon in* Schooner Under the Moon *and* Schooner with Icebergs *seems strange. The moon can often be seen 'on its back', but Wallis shows the moon the other way up. During the eclipse of 12th September 2015 the moon was visible just as Wallis portrayed it here. An eclipse of the moon also occurred in September 1876, at the time Wallis was crossing the North Atlantic aboard* Belle Aventure.

**To summarise the events of 1876 in chronological order we have documentary evidence of the following:**

| | |
|---|---|
| 2nd April | Wallis married Susan Ward at St Mary's Church, Penzance. |
| 24th April | Wallis aged 19 joins Westcountry schooner *Pride of the West* in Penzance. |
| 26th April | *Pride of the West* sailed from Penzance to Cadiz. |
| 8th May | *Pride of the West* arrived in Cadiz. |
| 12th May | *Pride of the West* sailed from Cadiz to St John's Newfoundland. |
| 10th June | *Pride of the West* arrived in St John's. |
| 24th June | *Pride of the West* sailed from St John's to Little Glace Bay, Nova Scotia. |
| 7th July | *Pride of the West* arrived in Little Glace Bay, Nova Scotia. Shipping officer, Little Glace Bay records: *One man discharged by mutual consent and re-shipped for passage to St. John. One man shipped for voyage. Also forwarded to St. John Newfoundland five men of the ship ... (indecipherable).* |
| 11th July | *Pride of the West* left Little Glace Bay. |
| 13th July | *Pride of the West* arrived in St John's, Newfoundland. |
| 31st July | Wallis left *Pride of the West* by mutual consent in St John's, Newfoundland. Mercantile Marine Office, St John's records: *I hereby certify that Anthony Benson and Alfred Wallis & Boatswain have been duly discharged at this port by mutual consent and the balance of the wages distributed to them in my presence.* |
| 7th August | Wallis joins *Belle Aventure* and sails from Newfoundland. |
| 9th November | Wallis discharged from *Belle Aventure* in Teignmouth. |

**Sailing Ship and a Lighthouse** (inscribed: Bellaventur of Brixham Larbordoor Iceburges)

Oil and pencil on card 10¾ x 15 in (27.3 x 38.1 cm) Private Collection

This is on the reverse of the painting on page 40.

**The Salt Cod Trade**

A number of authors have stated that Wallis worked in the Newfoundland cod fishery, but this is not so. The cod had been caught by Canadian fishermen. The ships Wallis served on were not involved in fishing, but were transporting cargoes of dried salt cod from Newfoundland to Europe.

Nevertheless it is worth describing this important fishery. Historically, the waters along the eastern coast of Canada and northeast America were rich fishing grounds. The Grand Banks are the most well-known of these particularly abundant fisheries. They are the meeting place of several major ocean currents: the Labrador Current, the St Lawrence Current and the Gulf Stream.

The Canadian fishing schooners that plied these waters were about 60-80 ft in length and crewed by ten to twelve men. Small rowing boats known as dories, which could be stacked inside each other on deck, were launched from the schooners. They were manned by one or two fishermen who would either jig for cod with handlines, or set longlines with hundreds of baited hooks, which were hauled, cleared, baited and reset throughout the day. The dories returned to the schooners where the fish were gutted, the head and backbone removed and the flesh cleaned. The freshly caught cod was then dispatched to the hold where it was packed; a layer of salt, a layer of fish and so on.

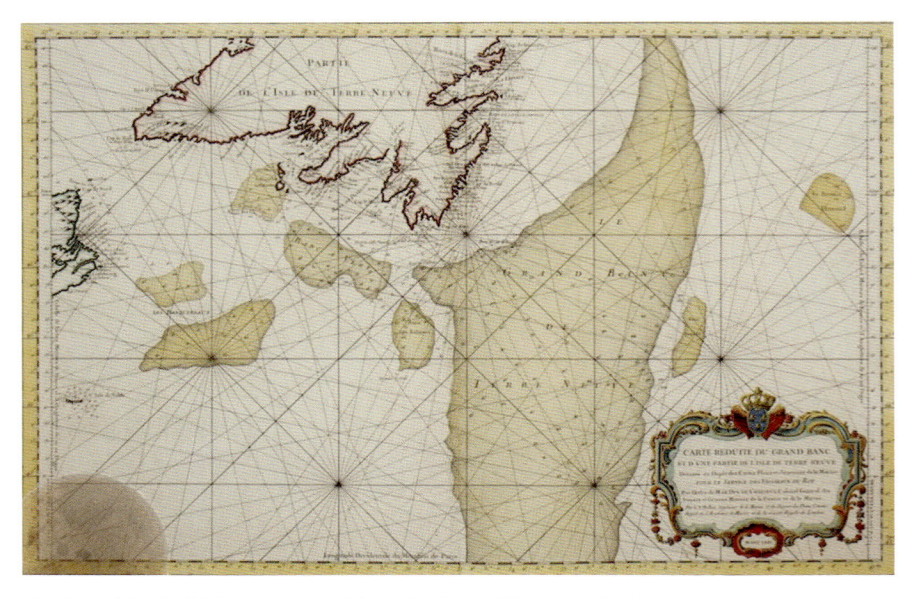

*The Grand Banks fishing grounds of Nova Scotia and Newfoundland.*

Working in this way, a fishing schooner would stay at sea for weeks - or until the hold was full - before returning to shore. Life aboard these ships was hard, and it was a particularly dangerous occupation for the men in the dories, for besides the rough seas and swells of the North Atlantic this was an area prone to frequent periods of dense fog, and if unable to find their way back to ship, men could be lost at sea. Others drowned when their 15ft dories, overloaded with fish, became swamped; the men in their heavy oilskins stood no chance of survival in the freezing waters. Many of the fishing grounds were located on major shipping routes so there was the additional danger that fishing schooners or dories could be run down by steamships.

*Photograph of Canadian fishing schooners.*
Photo: Maritime History Archive, Memorial University of Newfoundland

*"A Slack day on the Premises of George M. Barr"*
Photo: Maritime History Archive, Memorial University of Newfoundland
*A sea of masts on the waterfront at St John's, Newfoundland. The ironic title of this photograph highlights the intense activity involved in the thriving cod trade. Photographer, S.H. Parsons & Sons, St. John's.*

When the schooners returned, the fish was put ashore, washed and laid out on wooden structures known as flakes, to dry in the sun. If it rained, all the drying fish had to be brought in, a labour intensive process that involved women and children. Given good weather, the drying took between one and two weeks. Salting and drying was an effective way of preserving the cod, and it could be stored for many months provided it was kept dry. The sight of fish laid out to dry in the sun was a prominent feature of the many small settlements and harbours along these eastern coasts.

From the mid-nineteenth century, merchant sailing ships from all over Europe came to settlements in Newfoundland and other ports in Canada and north-eastern America for cargoes of salt cod. Vessels from south-west England, Wales and Denmark were particularly prominent in this trade. They returned over the Atlantic with their holds full, destined for the ports of Europe, especially to the Catholic countries of the Mediterranean where there was a practice of eating fish on Fridays. St John's in Newfoundland became the centre of the salt cod industry. *Pride of the West* and *Belle Aventure* were but two of the many ships involved in this well established trade, and Wallis was just one of the thousands of seamen who made the voyage across the Atlantic and back.

> *The fish caught on the inshore fishery are dried by the fisherman and their families in the small settlements to which they belong; the fish drying stages are the most conspicuous feature of every creekside settlement in Newfoundland. By the beginning of the 1870s West Country schooners had begun to appear in the trade, and it proved very profitable for them. In 1870 over fifty West Country schooners called at Harbour Grace. In the next ten years the European trade developed and it soon expanded to great proportions ... it was the greatest small ship trade of all time, and its importance to the history of the merchant schooners cannot be exaggerated.* [9]

**Sailing Vessels**

In his paintings, Wallis recalled life aboard the sailing ships and fishing boats that were a common sight around the coast in the nineteenth century. The various classes of sailing vessels were distinguished by their sail layout - that of lugger, sloop, ketch, schooner, brig, brigantine, barque, barquentine and full-rigged ship. Wallis was aware of this and he featured a great variety of sailing vessels in his paintings.

1. Lugger
2. Gaff Rigged Sloop/Cutter
3. Ketch
4. Schooner
5. Brig
6. Brigantine
7. Barquentine
8. Barque
9. Full-Rigged Ship

**Brigantine sailing past green fields**

Oil on card 16½ x 19¼ in (41.8 x 48.8 cm) Kettle's Yard, University of Cambridge

*In this and other paintings, Wallis exaggerates the scale of the ratlines - rope ladders going up the mast - which crew members could be called upon to climb at all times of day or night in all weathers to make sail adjustments using the reef points he shows on the sails.*

**Lugger and Two Sailing Ships Approaching a Port**
Private Collection

It is important to realise the spirit of enterprise that drove men to invest sufficient money to commission the building of a new ship and to sink their wealth in a speculative venture, the success of which was always dependent on weather. When things went well returns could be good, but this was an unpredictable business. Ships required constant maintenance, refits and repairs, besides the cost of wages for master and crew. There were times when they had to wait while a cargo was found and there was always the possibility that the ship could be damaged by collision, dismasted in a gale, or worse; sometimes ships simply disappeared at sea with everything lost - vessel, cargo and men.

In the westcountry, ships were built in harbours, creeks, coves, estuaries, on riversides and even on sheltered beaches all around the coast, using timber that was locally available or imported from Scandinavia and Canada.

Schooners usually carried four or five men, drawn from the area around their home port. Life aboard was hard; at times, seamen had to work in considerable discomfort and danger. The working day was inevitably long, and they could be called upon to work at any time of the day or night. When at sea, no matter what the weather, there were constant sail adjustments to be made, rigging and sails to be repaired and water to be pumped from the bilges. Frequently, all hands were required to take advantage of the wind to promote the fastest passage.

The food was basic. A coal stove in the galley was used for cooking, but in rough seas it was often impossible to get hot food for several days. In the event of accident or illness, only basic medical treatment was on hand - dispensed by fellow seamen.

When in port, the crew usually dealt with the cargo, discharging and loading. Seamen could be away at sea for many months. Without ship-to-shore contact, they were completely out of touch with land and their home ports.

**Grey Schooner**

Oil on card 10 x 19 in (25.4 x 48.3 cm) Pallant House Gallery

*This painting depicts the class of vessel that Wallis worked aboard, a Westcountry Schooner.*

**Brigantine with figurehead**

Oil and pencil on card 8 x 10¼ in (20.3 x 26 cm) Kettle's Yard, University of Cambridge

**Schooner and Lighthouse**

Oil on and pencil laid on card 7½ x 9 in (19 x 22.9 cm) Image courtesy of Sotheby's

**Black Boat**

Oil on card 9 x 11¾ in (23 x 29.8 cm) Image courtesy of Sotheby's

## Steamships

Besides the sailing ships that Wallis knew so well, a variety of steamships also feature in his paintings. Although the wind is free, sailing ships are wholly dependent on the weather. In time, steamships proved faster and more dependable, and sail was eventually replaced by steam.

Wallis would have seen steam-powered vessels when at sea, and during his days in St Ives steamships were a regular sight in the bay and called at the harbour and came to and from the port of Hayle; they were also a familiar sight in Penzance and Newlyn.

**Steamer**
Oil on card 3¾ x 8⅞ in (9.6 x 22.4 cm) Private Collection

**Steam**

Oil on card 5 x 10½ in (12.7 x 26.7 cm) Private Collection

*This painting is one side of a double-sided painting. Two steamships make their way through a stormy sea. Wallis shows one ship rolling away from us and the other towards us, giving a real feeling of the motion of the ships at sea in rough weather. How well this painting evokes the feeling expressed by John Masefield in his poem Cargoes:*

*Dirty British coaster with a salt-caked smokestack*
*Butting through the Channel in the mad March days,*
*With a cargo of Tyne coal,*
*Road-rail, pig-lead,*
*Firewood, iron-ware, and cheap tin trays.*

**Steamship in a Rough Sea**
Private Collection

**Two Steamships**
Collection Holly Johnson
*This painting evokes my own memories of fishing off Falmouth in winter, and the ship on the horizon reminds me of how, in rough weather, passing vessels in the distance would appear and disappear from view.*

# Mount's Bay

Mount's Bay takes its name from the presence of St Michael's Mount. Wallis clearly knew the bay well and painted it many times, depicting the whole of the bay with its significant geographical features.

In the top right corner of this painting, to which Wallis gave the lengthy title *'Penzance Harbour, Newlyn Harbour, Mousall Island, The Mount, Porthleven and Mullion Near Lizard. The one Entrin the harbour is a Revenue Cutter from Penzance,'* the Lizard Light appears. This is an important lighthouse marking a treacherous set of rocks and tidal currents at the most southerly point of Cornwall and mainland Britain.

To the left of the lighthouse, the painting follows the coast of the Lizard Peninsula and shows two towns with harbours, Mullion and Porthleven. At the top centre of the painting is St Michael's Mount with the welcoming arms of its harbour. In the top left, the town and harbour of Penzance is shown with its inner harbour and road bridge and, in the corner, St Mary's Church. The cutter is sailing into Newlyn Harbour, with its lighthouse at the end of the south pier. Along the bottom of the painting is the south east coast of Penwith, with Mousehole and St Clement's Island, and further on, Lamorna or Penberth.

Revenue cutters were impressive sailing vessels built to withstand any weather and ride out gales at sea. They were initially employed in chasing smugglers, and later in general customs duties.

This small painting represents the whole of Mount's Bay with its lights, harbours and rocks. Its features are those significant to a seaman. It is a map of the sea.

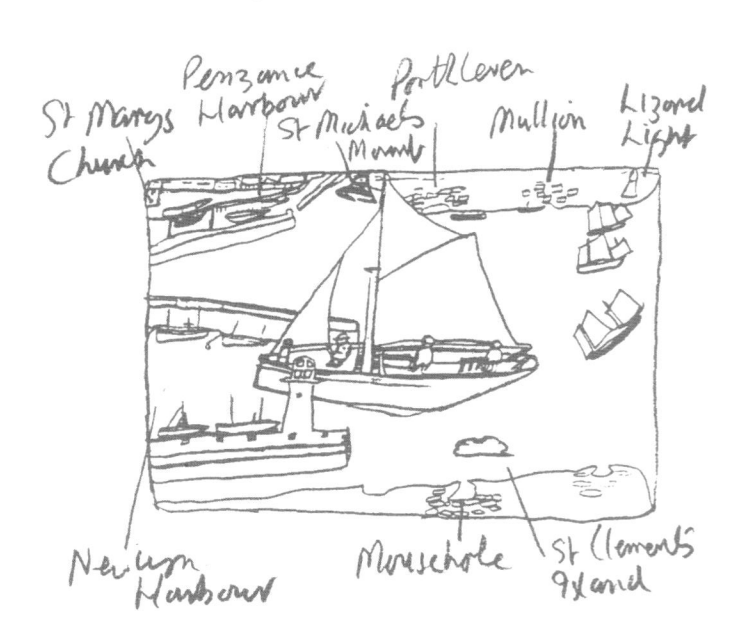

Penzance Harbour, Newlyn Harbour, Mousall Island, The Mount, Porthleven, and Mullion nr. Lizard. The one Entren the harbour is a revenew Cutter from Penzance.
Oil on card 8 x 10 in (20.3 x 25.4 cm) Cornwall Council

*The gear pole beacon photographed in the 1930s*

**Mount's Bay with St Michael's Mount**

Oil and crayon on board 11 x 15¾ in (27.9 x 40 cm) Private Collection

*A small but significant detail reveals Wallis's understanding of the hazards of sailing in Mount's Bay. Just off the shore of Penzance are low rocks, which are covered at high tide. The hazard was marked by a metal pole topped with a sphere. To the left in this painting, Wallis has shown one of the rocks with its mark.*

**Mount's Bay - Five Ships**

Oil on card 17¼ x 21¾ in (44 x 55.5 cm) Kettle's Yard, University of Cambridge

*In times of gales, Mount's Bay provides an effective shelter; even today, power-driven vessels seek refuge here while waiting for the wind to subside before continuing their voyage round Land's End or the Lizard. This painting surely represents five sailing ships sheltering in Mount's Bay in a gale; the ships are carrying only minimal sail because of the strength of the wind.*

*Gibson photograph of St Michael's Mount.*
Photo: Penlee House Gallery & Museum, Penzance/The Gibson Archive
*Part of the town of Marazion can be seen in the foreground.*

**A Mackerel Lugger in Mount's Bay**
Oil and pencil on card laid on panel 8⅞ x 8¾ in (22.4 x 22.2 cm) Image courtesy of Christie's
*A Cornish lugsail fishing boat sails into Mount's Bay, passing Lizard Point with its lighthouse. The harbours of Mullion and Porthleven are seen, and St Michael's Mount is featured in the top left of the painting with a harbour and cottages at the bottom; at the top, the castle is marked by the flag, and trees and wildlife are seen on the Lizard peninsula.*

**Penzance Harbour**

Oil on card 12 x 18 in (30.5 x 45.7 cm) Kettle's Yard, University of Cambridge

*Steamships make their way across Mount's Bay to Penzance Harbour. Wallis remembers the inner harbour and the Ross Bridge, which is still in use and is shown at the bottom right of this painting. St Michael's Mount is on the top left and on the top right is the Lizard Light.*

**St Michael's Mount Harbour**

Oil on board 14½ x 18 in (36.8 x 45.7 cm) University of Essex

*St Michael's Mount with its castle, chapel and the arms of its harbour are at the top left of this painting of Mount's Bay. On the left of St Michael's Mount, the town of Marazion, and to the right of the Mount, the Lizard Peninsula with Porthleven, Mullion and the Lizard Light. At the bottom left of the painting is Penzance (or possibly Newlyn) Harbour. Between the harbour and St Michael's Mount, rocks are shown. Again, Wallis clearly knew that these rocks, which lie off Penzance, are a hazard to shipping as they are covered at high tide. Along the left of the painting Wallis shows the GWR railway line that runs to and from Penzance, and at the bottom right, St Clement's Island, which lies off Mousehole.*

*The painting represents the whole of Mount's Bay with a fishing lugger and sailing boats returning to port. Wallis made his paintings on his kitchen table. He would envisage the scene from above and, turning the painting or moving around it, paint it from different viewpoints. Here, the quays and vessels of this harbour, bottom left, are seen from all four sides of the painting.*

**Sailing Ships and Two Steamers**

Oil on board 10 x 19¼ in (25.4 x 48.9 cm)
Kettle's Yard, University of Cambridge

*A fleet of Cornish fishing luggers sail towards Penzance or possibly Newlyn harbour; the lighthouse at the end of South Pier is shown. (Both harbours have inner harbours with lighthouses on the south pier). On the right, two steamships follow the fishing boats into Mount's Bay.*

Map of south west Cornwall

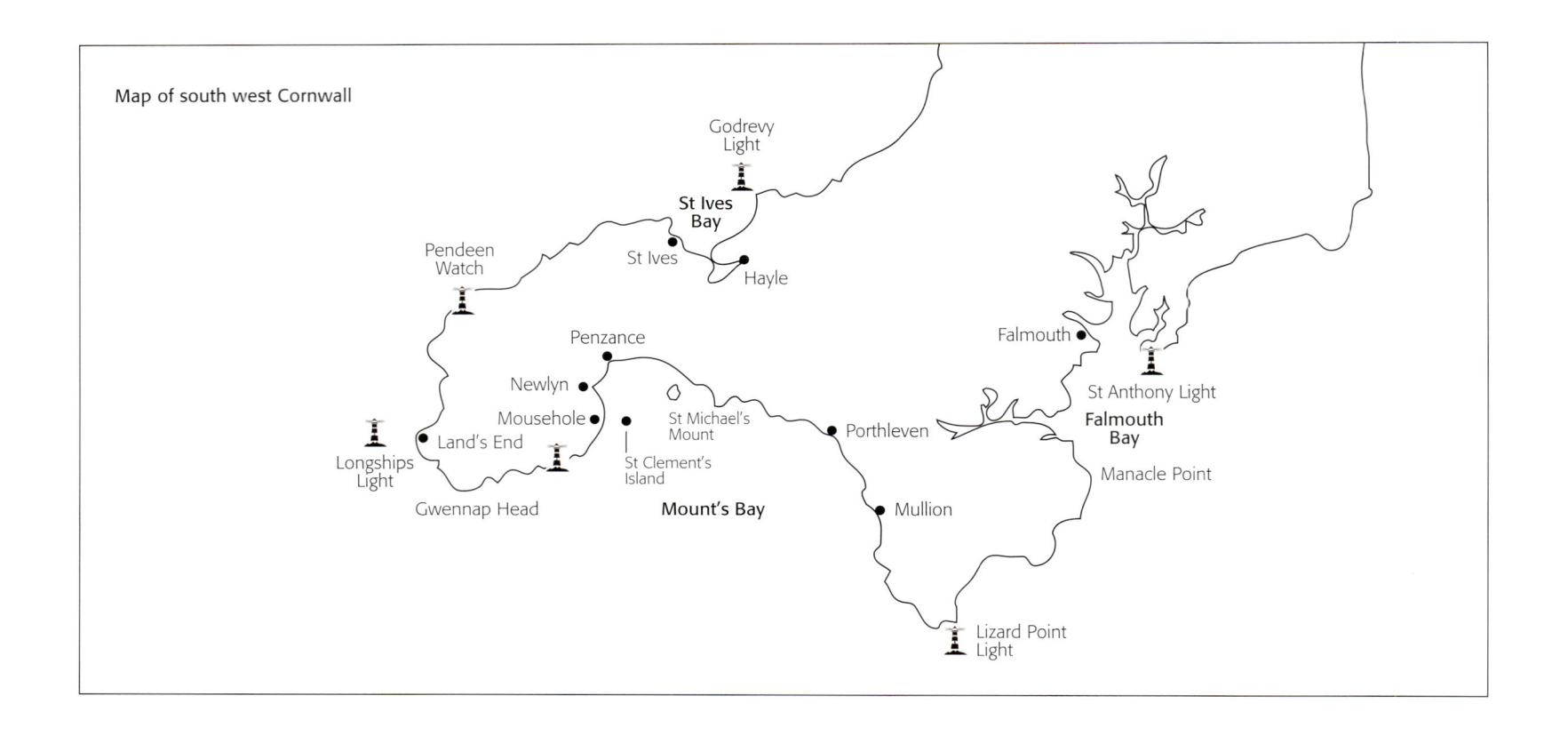

**Four Sailing Boats**
Private Collection

Newlyn Harbour

Private Collection

## Golden Light

The fact that Wallis has named this ship and signed his name across the top of the painting indicates that he knew and perhaps worked aboard the vessel. If so, this would also account for an unusual painting in the Kettle's Yard collection, which seems to show the Avon Gorge and Brunel's Clifton suspension bridge. The River Avon leads from the city of Bristol to the sea. In that painting, the coast and beaches of south Wales can be seen in the distance across the Bristol Channel.

The wooden schooner *Golden Light* had an elliptical stern, as Wallis has recorded in this painting. For many years, the ship took a triangular course - carrying smelting slag from Penzance to Bristol where it was used for glass-making, then sailing to Newport and returning to Penzance with coal from the Welsh mines. At other times, the vessel carried copper ore from the Cornish mines to be smelted in Wales, again returning with Welsh coal, much of it to be used in the pumping engines of Cornish mines.

**Ravine with Estuary**
Oil on card 12½ x 19½ in (32 x 49.5 cm)
Kettle's Yard, University of Cambridge
*Bristol Channel with Suspension Bridge.*

**Golden Light**, *St Marys, Isles of Scilly*
Photo: Royal Institution of Cornwall

Golden Light *and* Alliance *washed ashore in Penzance 1886*
Royal Institution of Cornwall

*On 7th December 1886, in a south-southwesterly gale,* Golden Light *went ashore at Penzance, along with the ketch* Alliance*, owned by Joe Denley of Penzance. The lifeboat rescued five men and a dog from* Golden Light*, after which the vessel was bought and refitted by another local merchant who used her in the coasting trade.*

**The Golden Light penzance** (inscribed with title)
Oil on board 7½ x 9½ in (19 x 24.1 cm) Private Collection

### Alpha and Beta

Sven Berlin names two Penzance vessels that Wallis worked on: *Alpha* and *Omega*, owned, he says, by a man called Beasley. There were indeed two sailing vessels, named *Alpha* and *Beta* (rather than *Omega*), registered in Penzance during Wallis's days as a seaman, both owned by a 'George Bazeley'. Given that Berlin took this information from conversations with people who knew Wallis, this was an understandable mistake.

George Bazeley & Sons of the Albert Stores, Penzance, were prominent merchants and ship owners with wide business interests. As well as dealing in groceries and provisions, they had invested in a flour producing steam mill for the grain they imported, and were involved in mechanical ice production for the fishing industry. With his sons, George Bazeley also owned a number of steamships, which traded as the Little Western Steamship Company.

Bazeley acquired *Beta* (official no.68556) and the ship was registered in Penzance in 1875. The crew agreements covering the period December 1875 - July 1876 show that the ship was employed in the coasting trade, and visited ports such as Cardiff, Swansea, London and Chatham. *Beta* carried flour to the family's warehouses in Cardiff, and brought back grain, groceries and coal.

Later, Bazeley acquired another ship, which he renamed *Alpha* (official no.51302), and registered in Penzance in 1877. The crew agreements covering voyages from October 1877 to 1879 show that the vessel was employed in the home trade and visited, amongst other places, the Channel Islands, Antwerp, Palermo and Gallipoli.

The ship's records for these vessels are available only for a limited number of years. So far, no crew agreement has been found to establish that Wallis worked aboard, but the fact that both *Alpha* and *Beta* were working and registered in Penzance from 1875 substantiates Berlin's statement.

*19th century photograph*
Photo: Penlee House Gallery & Museum, Penzance/The Gibson Archive
*Three sailing ships leave Penzance.*
*George Bazeley's schooner* Alpha *is on the right.*

**The Schooner the Beata, Penzance, Mount's Bay and Newlyn Harbour** (inscribed with title)

Oil on board 15¾ x 19⅞ in (40 x 50.5 cm) Private Collection

*Wallis depicts Mount's Bay. The schooner* Beta *sails across the bay. The buildings on the left closely resemble those on the seafront at Penzance. Wallis has named the ship in this painting, which adds support to Berlin's statement that he worked aboard.*

*Mosques seen from the water's edge of the Bosphorus, Turkey*

## Other Voyages

Kettle's Yard holds two paintings that indicate Alfred Wallis may have sailed to the Mediterranean and the Black Sea.

Some ships sailing to the Mediterranean went through the Bosphorus to the Black and Azov Seas to collect grain from Ukraine. This was a regular and significant trade route in the nineteenth century, and the Black Sea ports became the granary of industrialised Europe.

The painting entitled *Shoreline* is out of the ordinary in the Wallis canon; it has a foreign feel. What are the buildings on the shore? The building with the tower appears to be a mosque and the tower its minaret. Several mosques are clearly visible along the shore in the Bosphorus. For Wallis, this view of the shore from a ship surely represents a memory of a striking view in a foreign land.

**Shoreline**
Oil and pencil on card 4 x 8½ in (10.1 x 21.3 cm) Kettle's Yard, University of Cambridge

**St Michael's Mount**
Oil on card 10½ x 13 in (26.6 x 33 cm)
Kettle's Yard, University of Cambridge
Portland *and* Gibraltar *have also been suggested as titles for this painting,*

It is worth remembering that although Wallis inscribed titles on some of his paintings, a great many titles were created by the people who bought them, some of whom were mistaken about the subject of their painting. This could have been the case with the work known as *St Michael's Mount*. It has also been suggested that this painting represents Gibraltar or Portland.

The painting looks unlike any of Wallis's other depictions of St Michael's Mount, and indeed appears quite unlike the Mount itself. It does seem to depict an island, but it includes very specific architectural details in the rows of Roman arches, some of which are built on a slope. Similar architectural features can be seen in buildings overlooking the port of Valetta, Malta.

*As well as being a major British naval base, Valetta was a very common port of call for British merchant shipping, including vessels in the Black Sea grain trade, where they could re-stock on provisions and water.* [10]

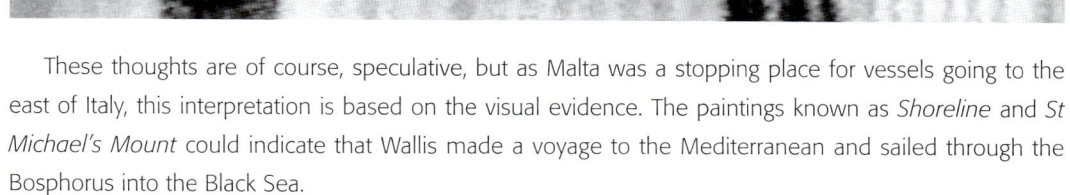

These thoughts are of course, speculative, but as Malta was a stopping place for vessels going to the east of Italy, this interpretation is based on the visual evidence. The paintings known as *Shoreline* and *St Michael's Mount* could indicate that Wallis made a voyage to the Mediterranean and sailed through the Bosphorus into the Black Sea.

Given the two decades that Alfred Wallis spent working as a seaman, it is possible that his name will yet be found on other articles of agreement. His practice of inscribing the name of ships he had worked aboard in paintings may also provide a lead to further discoveries.

*Waterfront buildings; Valetta harbour, Malta*

# Falmouth

Falmouth is the third-largest natural harbour in the world and it is by far the largest port in Cornwall. Wallis knew the area well and in his paintings he recalls the waterways, landscape and vessels associated with it.

The painting *Two ships and steamer sailing past a port - Falmouth and St. Anthony lighthouse* features the south coast of Cornwall between Falmouth and Penzance. In his imagination, Wallis looks down upon Falmouth Bay east of Lizard Point. On the left, behind the lighthouse, is Mount's Bay with St Michael's Mount; the town and harbour of Penzance are seen in the distance. The lighthouse is the Lizard Light. Along the coast to the right is a group of rocks called the Manacles, a notorious hazard for shipping and marked by a buoy. Further on is the mouth of the Fal and the town of Falmouth; two Cornish lug-sail fishing boats are seen sailing west. The features important to the seaman have remained in Wallis's memory to be recorded here in paint forty or fifty years later.

**Two Sailing Boats and a Lugger**
Oil and pencil on card 5¼ x 8¼ in (13.3 x 21 cm)
Image courtesy of Sotheby's

*Gaff-rigged sailing vessels were a common sight around the coast in Wallis's day. Several classes of vessel with this rig were associated with Falmouth, from the smaller Falmouth Quay Punts and Falmouth Working Boats (Oyster Dredgers) to the larger Revenue and Customs Cutters, as well as Westcountry Sailing Barges that carried cargoes to nearby ports and worked the upper reaches of the Fal.*

**Two ships and a steamer sailing past a port - Falmouth and St. Anthony lighthouse**

Oil on card 10½ x 16 in (26.3 x 40.9 cm)
Kettle's Yard, University of Cambridge

**Black Boat with Fort**

Oil on card 13 x 20 in (33 x 508 cm) Private Collection

*During his lifetime Wallis witnessed the decline of the age of sail and the increasing presence of steam-powered vessels. Perhaps this painting shows some awareness of this.*
*As for the location, this could be the mouth of the Fal and the fort, bristling with guns, Pendennis Castle, built by Henry VIII in 1540-42 at a time when defences were placed around the coast to protect Britain from invasion. If so, the top right corner represents the entrance to the Helford River and, at the top of the painting, the Lizard Peninsula. In the distance, a sailing ship is seen off the Helford, while the main subject of the painting, a black steamship with an elliptical stern makes its way towards the port of Falmouth, smoke streaming from its large funnel.*
*As inscribed verso it was given as a Christmas present by Barbara Hepworth to Denis Mitchell in 1957.*

*Nestor*

Because of its location, Falmouth was often the first port of call for ships sailing to Britain after a long voyage. Before the age of ship-to-shore communication, ships were out of touch with their owners for long periods when at sea, and on their return to Britain would anchor at Falmouth to collect orders informing them of the next port at which the vessel was to discharge or collect cargo. The phrase 'Falmouth for Orders' thus became part of maritime history.

In the latter part of the nineteenth century, a regular seasonal trade brought rice from Burma to Britain. In 1882 and 1883, over a dozen vessels in that year carrying rice called at Falmouth for orders. One of these was the iron-hulled German sailing ship *Nestor* - the largest vessel to have visited the port during those years. Fox's Arrivals Book records *Nestor*'s presence in Falmouth on two occasions. On 30th August 1882, the ship arrived from Rangoon with a cargo of rice, and the following year came from Rangoon to Falmouth, again with rice, eventually to be discharged in London on 19th September.

This painting enables us to date Wallis's presence in Falmouth to August 1882 or September 1883. This large ship was obviously an impressive sight. In his painting, Wallis shows *Nestor* passing Dover bound for London.

**Nestor**

Private Collection

**Tugboat**

Private Collection

*Steam-powered tugboats associated with the docks were an iconic sight on the Falmouth waterways in the 19th and 20th centuries. In this painting, so full of energy, Wallis remembers the details of the superstructure of the tugboat.*

*Tugboat* St Agnes.
*A later evolution of the tugboats that Wallis recalled, Falmouth steam tugboat* St Agnes *was built 1925. There were several of these vessels, all named after Cornish saints, working in Falmouth in the 1960s when I was an art student there in the 1960s.*

**A River Fal**

Oil on board 8 x 11¾ in (22.4 x 29.8 cm) Private Collection

**Two Boats Moving Past A Big House**

Oil on card 15 x 14¾ in (38 x 37.3 cm)
Kettle's Yard, University of Cambridge

*The landscape in this painting closely resembles the shore opposite Falmouth Docks; a sailing boat and a steamship head for Falmouth, passing houses in the town of Flushing, where the gardens reach the water's edge.*

**Fishing Boat With a Grey Sail**
Oil and pencil on card
6½ x 7½ in (16.5 x 19 cm)
Image courtesy of Sotheby's

*19th century photograph. Westcountry Sailing Barge* Sweet May *in Falmouth Bay.*

There are many gaff-rigged (fore-and-aft rigged, controlled by a spar (pole) called the gaff) sailing vessels associated with the waterways of Falmouth. To this day, Falmouth working boats dredge for oysters under sail in the Fal, in an area of deep water known as Carrick Roads. Some boats of this class, and modern replicas, are still a common sight on the Fal, and are raced regularly at weekends in summer and autumn. In Wallis's day Westcountry sailing barges were another commonplace class of gaff-rigged vessel seen on the Fal. Large ships in the docks would discharge cargo onto these barges for delivery to the shallow upper reaches of the river and along the coast.

'Many of the Coombe men combined growing plums with oyster dredging and fishing, but several owned sailing barges. Coombe was ideally placed for these barge owners as the deep draft of many sailing ships meant they could not sail up to Truro let alone to hamlets such as Tresillian or Ruan Lanihorne. So cargoes would be offloaded into smaller barges which would be sailed or "poled" if there was no wind. In addition these barges might carry barley to local malthouses, or coal or limestone to local limekilns. In addition, they often carried stone out to sailing ships who had discharged their cargo to act as ballast. These barges were known as "inside" barges, were between 40 to 50 feet in length, had a beam of 13 to 15 feet, and a draft of about 4 or 5 feet. They could carry cargoes of between 25 to 30 tons. The barges were gaff rigged and set a large mainsail, usually of a red ochre colour, but did not have a topmast or topsail. They also had a bowsprit and carried a foresail. Generally they were crewed by two men but perhaps three if a cargo had to be loaded or discharged. The barges were essentially sailing craft but when the wind failed they could also be "poled"'.
(Peeps into the Past - A history of Coombe in photos *by Nigel Baker)*

*19th century photographs of Westcountry Sailing Barges.*
Photos: Private Collection

**Gaff-rigged sailing boat with smaller vessels**

Oil on board 8 x 8 in (20 x 20 cm) Private Collection

*In this painting the central sailing ship has great presence; with such a limited palette Wallis makes effective use of the colour of the board.*

**Fishing Boat Off The Coast**

Oil on board 14½ x 14½ in (36.8 x 36.8 cm) Private Collection

*Walking or sailing south along the coast from Flushing brings one to Trefusis Point and Carrick Roads. The landscape in this painting and in* Four Sailing Ships *closely resembles this part of the coast.*

**Four Sailing Ships**

Oil and pencil on board 11 x 12¾ in (27.9 x 32.4 cm) Private Collection

**Grey Sailing Ship and Small Boat**

Oil on card 11¾ x 19¾ in (30 x 50 cm)
Kettle's Yard, University of Cambridge

*Wallis sometimes painted on both sides of a board.*
*This painting is verso of* Boats Under Saltash Bridge.

**Three Sailing Vessels on a River**

Private Collection

*The painting* Three Sailing Vessels on a River *depicts gaff-rigged sailing ships. Although similar in rig to Falmouth working boats, the craft in this painting seem larger. They have ratlines on the masts for the crew to climb in order to make adjustments to the sails. Such Westcountry sailing barges were used to transport cargo from the larger ships that came into Falmouth to the shallow points of discharge on the upper reaches of the Fal, Truro River and along the coast. The painting shows sheltered wooded areas along the waterway, and a small quay, possibly Mylor, Point, Devoran or perhaps Roundwood Quay - the latter being a particular centre for these vessels, which were also built there. The fact that Wallis also painted similar vessels passing trees in blossom shows that he knew these waters and recalled this unusual sight, associated with Coombe or Kea where apple and plum orchards are visible from the river. Larger, deeper-draft vessels visiting Falmouth Docks and Carrick Roads did not ordinarily visit these places; one could speculate that Wallis became familiar with these waterways through working on Westcountry sailing barges. An inscription on the back of this painting reads: 'To Stevan and Gwinneth their marriage 1937 from Jim Ede painting by Alfred Wallis'.* [11]

**Sailing Ship and Orchard**
Oil on card 8½ x 8¼ in (21.8 x 21.1 cm)
Kettle's Yard, University of Cambridge

*A gaff-rigged vessel passes trees in blossom. The scene is reminiscent of spring in the area around Coombe with its apple and pear orchards, and nearby Kea known for Kea plums. These places are on the sheltered upper reaches of the Fal and this and similar paintings are surely based on Wallis's personal observations.*

'Coombe was best known for its "Plum Gardens" … The source of the Kea plum, a dark blue damson-like plum, is not known but it had gained an enviable reputation for making wonderful jam. Helston had its Kea Plum Fair each September. Early tourists would come in May to view the blossom, and again in September to see the trees straining under the weight of the fruit.'
(*Peeps into the Past - A history of Coombe in photos* by Nigel Baker)

# Fishing

Wallis eventually gave up deep sea voyages to work as a fisherman with the Newlyn and Mousehole fleets. The fishing industry in this area was thriving. Berlin mentioned that Wallis worked aboard a boat called *Flying Scud* and made trips around the coast of Britain following shoals of herring.

The artist made a great many paintings of Cornish lug-sailed fishing boats and he painted *Flying Scud* many times. A first-class lugger from Newlyn, this vessel was registered in Penzance (Port Register no. PZ11, official no. 50713, registered tonnage 16-17, length 45.5ft). The owners and masters were Job Kelynack of Newlyn and William Badcock. First registered in 1867, the lugger fished until 1893 before being broken up. The half-yearly crew sheets of 1873-6 state that the boat was 'constantly employed in fishing' and had a crew of seven.

Alfred Wallis was in extraordinary company when he worked aboard *Flying Scud*. Kelynack and Badcock had been members of the crew of *Mystery*, a half-decked, 33ft Mount's Bay lugger, which sailed from Penzance to Melbourne, Australia in 1854/55. This famous and remarkable voyage took 116 days. Kelynack and Badcock stayed in Australia until 1859, when they returned to Cornwall.

Flying Scud - *PZ 11 1867-1893*

*The Kelynack–Badcock link was further strengthened in 1867 when the two men had a new lugger built at Newlyn. The spring mackerel fishery out of Mount's Bay had boomed in the years following the completion of the Albert bridge over the Tamar in 1858. Fresh fish could now be whisked away to London and other major inland markets by train, while Lowestoft and other east coast boats were participating in the fishery in ever increasing numbers. Local fishermen were not slow to take advantage of new markets either, and several first-class mackerel drivers were built in the mid-1860s. One of these was the 16-ton lugger* Flying Scud, *registered at Penzance Custom house on 14 March 1867, just in time for the new mackerel season which had commenced about a fortnight earlier.* [12]

**PZ 11 Flying Scud of Newlyn** (inscribed with title)
Image courtesy of Will's Lane Gallery, St Ives
*Painted on an envelope and inscribed.*
*What life and energy this piece has! The lugger seems to speed across the surface of the painting.*

*PZ11 Penzance*

Photo: Penlee House Gallery & Museum, Penzance

*This is the lugsail fishing boat that Alfred Wallis worked aboard. Photographed in Penzance Harbour in the 1880s, the crew are raising the foresail of PZ11* Flying Scud *before leaving the harbour.*

**PZ 11 Boat With Fishermen Letting Out Nets**

Oil on card 3¼ x 7 in (8 x 18 cm) Kettle's Yard, University of Cambridge

*Recalling his fishing days, this painting of PZ 11* Flying Scud *shows Wallis's considerable knowledge the working methods of Cornish fishing boats of the period. The detail in the painting conveys the artist's understanding of his subject, which must have come from first-hand experience.*

*The painting called* Boat with Fishermen Letting Out Nets *is in the Kettle's Yard collection, and was presumably given this title by Jim Ede. However, it actually depicts a fishing boat hauling in its nets.*

- The main sail was taken down and the mast stepped to reduce rolling, making the boat more stable while hauling the nets.
- A ring on the mast, known as a traveller, was attached to the sail, enabling it to be hauled up the mast and set.
- The mizzen sail was set to keep the boat facing the wind.
- These boats were always crewed by seven men, or 'six men and a boy' as sometimes recorded.
- These boats had a net hold and a separate fish hold, as shown.
- The steam-driven capstan on the deck was used to haul in the foot rope.
- A fisherman in the bow would untie the leashes that attach the foot ropes to the net.
- The cork floats were attached to the top of the net.
- The ship's rowing boat was carried on deck.

**Ship with seven men, net and gulls**

Oil on card 7½ x 11 in (18.7 x 27.9 cm) Kettle's Yard, University of Cambridge

*A lugger, with the crew hauling in nets laden with fish. The mizzen is set to keep the boat facing the wind. Cornish fishing boats worked their gear on the starboard side, as shown here. The main mast was lowered when hauling the nets in order to reduce the amount the boat rolled. The outriggers on the stern of the pilchard and mackerel boats were set on the port side, as Wallis has depicted. Scavenging gulls often congregate around fishing boats when nets are being hauled.*

**PZ 11**
Private Collection

*On the reverse of this painting is inscribed: 'This is the number That I was in about 65 years ago i was sea sick i never Eat anything on Till we got to scarBro from newlyn'. Clearly this provides further evidence of Wallis's connection with* Flying Scud *and supports Berlin's idea that he took part in herring fishing with the Cornish fishing fleet.*

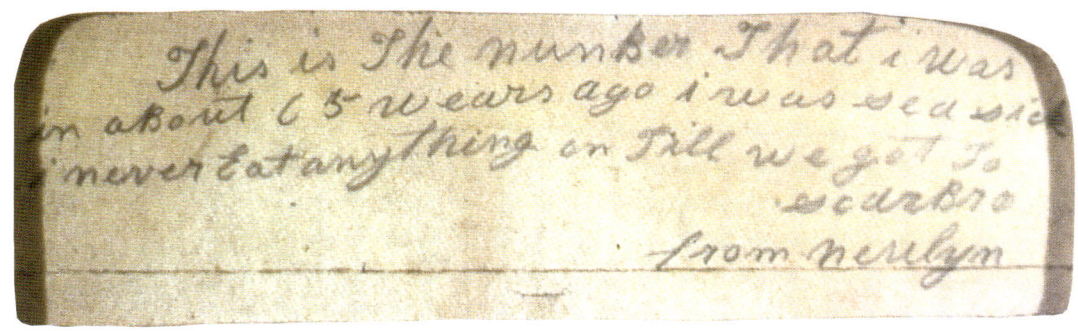

**Inscription on reverse of PZ11**
Private Collection

**The Flying Scud, Newlyn** (inscribed with title)
Private Collection

*19th century photo of St Ives luggers.*
Photo: Morrab Library, Penzance

**PZ 11 Mount's Bay**

Oil on wood 14¼ x 18⅛ in (35.9 x 46 cm) Private Collection

*In this painting Alfred Wallis recalls Flying Scud returning to Newlyn with its nets on deck.*
*The boat is followed by a flock of gulls. On the left of the painting is St. Michael's Mount.*

*Fishing fleet on the shore at Newlyn.*
Photo: Morrab Library, Penzance

### Cornish Fishing

The pilchard and mackerel drivers were an interesting class of fishing boat peculiar to the west country in the last century. These vessels appear in many of Wallis's paintings and understanding them and their fishing methods gives us a further insight into his life and work.

The West Cornwall lugger appears as two main types: the 28-30 ft pilchard drivers and the more substantial 45-48 ft mackerel drivers. Both were rigged with lug sails and distinctive outriggers at the stern.

### Pilchard Drivers

The pilchard drivers worked around the coast of Cornwall with drift nets, which were shot at dusk. The boat and the nets, which hung down in the water like a curtain, drifted along with the tide. During the night, the fish that swam into the net were caught by the gills. In the early morning, or when the net was full, the fishermen hauled it over a roller on the starboard side of the boat. They shook out the fish onto the deck while the cleared net was being stored in the net room below. There was often conflict between the two methods of catching pilchards, and seine fishermen working close inshore (described later) said that drift net fishing split up the shoals and drove the pilchards away - hence they called these boats 'drivers'.

### Mackerel Drivers

The mackerel season started in February or March and lasted until the end of June. The early season started with boats leaving port and sailing sometimes a hundred miles west of the Wolf Rock to meet migrating shoals. Like the pilchard boats, they would shoot their nets at dusk and drift with them. The foremast was lowered to stop the boat rolling and the mizzen sail set to keep her to wind. Their drift nets were many fathoms long and usually seven fathoms deep. The nets hung from the surface of the water and caught the mackerel by the gills, but unlike pilchards and herring, they could not be shaken out, and each fish had to be taken from the mesh by hand. The boats had a crew of six or seven men.

There was often a race between boats back to port, the first to land their catch getting the better price. Cork buoys were set at intervals along the head rope. The business of fishing has always been a dangerous one and for these small vessels particularly so, reliant only on sail and without the benefit of weather forecasts, the loss of a fishing boat and all aboard in a gale was a common occurrence. There was also the constant danger, particularly at night, of being run down by larger steamships.

# Wick

Fraserburgh

Peterhead

## SCOTLAND

NORTH SEA

Grangemouth
Berwick
Bowling

July

August

Hartlepool
Whitby
Scarborough

September

Ardglass

Peel
Isle of Man

## IRELAND

IRISH SEA

Howth

August

Wicklow
Arklow

July

Yarmouth
Lowestoft

## ENGLAND

WALES

Plymouth

ENGLISH CHANNEL

St Ives

September

### Herring Fishing

When the mackerel season ended in June, the big mackerel boats then put aboard their herring nets and set off to fish far away from home in the Irish Sea and the North Sea. At the height of this fishing in the 1880s about 100 boats with 800 men and boys left St Ives each June. They landed their fish in Ireland at ports such as Arklow, Wicklow, Howth, Kilkeel and Ardglass, and also on the Isle of Man. Many of the fish landed in these ports were smoked and made into kippers. The luggers then headed for the Forth and Clyde Canal, with its thirty locks through which the fishermen towed their boats. This took them across Scotland, where they then set to fish the North Sea, working their way down the east coast following the shoals of herring. They landed at such ports as Berwick, Hartlepool, Whitby and Scarborough.

> *On Sunday the Cornishmen stayed in harbour and, although far away from their chapels in the cobbled streets of Newlyn, Mousehole and St Ives, they often met together for their own services. They praised the Lord in harmony, singing their favourite Methodist hymns and the local people would be moved by their fervent worship, remembering it long afterwards. The herring season ended in about mid-September and the Cornish luggers raced each other home, down the North Sea and through the English Channel. The speed record was held by the* Lloyd *(port no. SS5) which, in 1902, sailed the 600 miles from Scarborough to St Ives in fifty hours. She landed herring in St Ives that had been caught in the North Sea two days before. The* Leading Star *(SS615) and* Johanna *(SS601) sailed from Scarborough to St Ives in fifty-five hours, and the* Nellie Jane *(SS503) in fifty-six hours. The safe return of the boats also brought thanksgiving services at the local churches, especially at the Mariners Chapel where the Harvest of the Sea services also expressed gratitude for the safe return.* [13]

From the 1880s to the mid-1930s, there was also an autumn herring fishery along the north coast of Cornwall. Herring were caught in St Ives Bay and all along the north coast of Cornwall, off Newquay, Padstow and Port Isaac. In a good season, many tons of fish were caught. In one period of just four days in 1892, over 1,000 tons of herring were sent off by train from St Ives.

Besides being sold fresh, some of the fish were turned into kippers. Scottish girls regularly came down to St Ives by train to help clean and pack the fish.

*St Ives Lugger.*
Photo: Morrab Library, Penzance

**Four Luggers in a Row**
Oil on board 5 x 13 in (12.7 x 33 cm) Private Collection

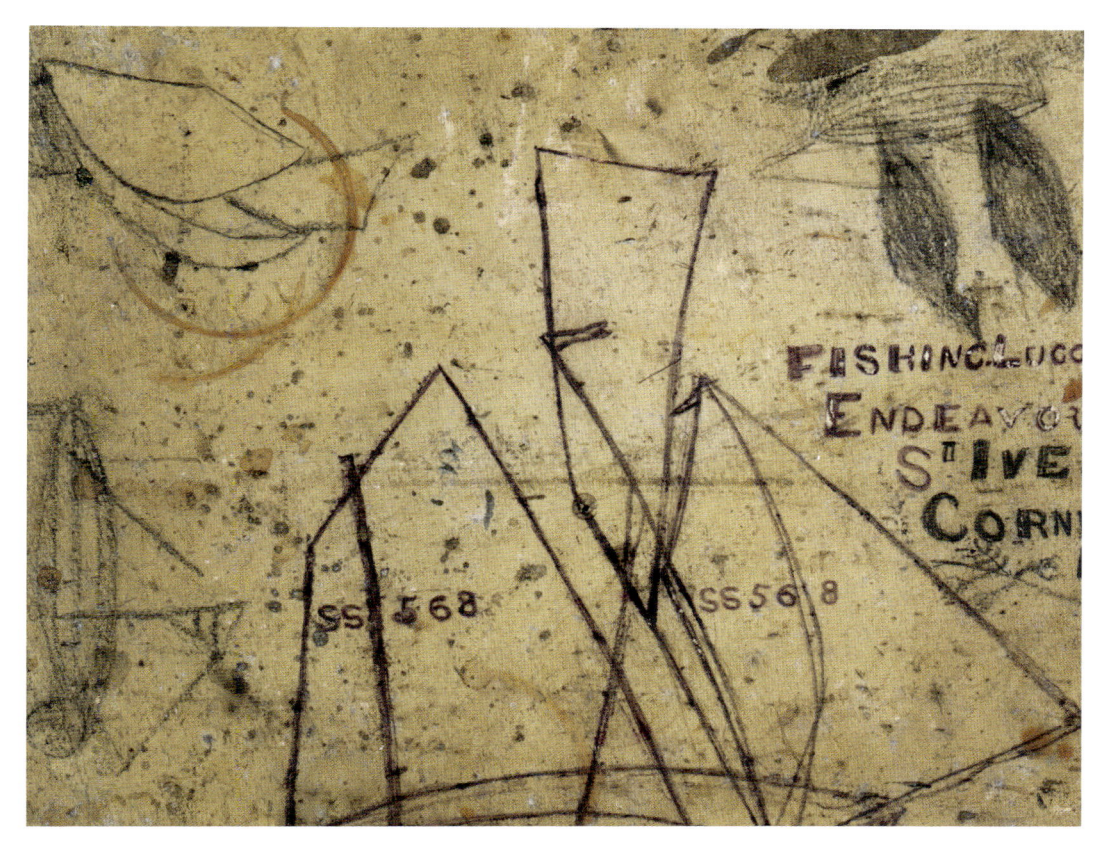

**Fishing Lugger and Sketches of Boats**
Pencil and crayon on card 10 x 13¼ in (25.7 x 33.7 cm) Kettle's Yard, University of Cambridge

*SS568 Endeavour.*
Photo: St Ives Archive

*The Crew of* Endeavour
*In the Kettle's Yard Collection there is a crayon/pencil drawing of the sails of the fishing boat* Endeavour *SS568, a boat Wallis would have been familiar with in St Ives. This photograph depicts the crew of* Endeavour *described as the youngest crew to have sailed north. Two years later the skipper was washed overboard and drowned.*

*Fishing Lugger on Penzance promenade beach taken in the 1870s.*

Photo: Reg Watkiss Collection

*The fishermen have hoisted the lugger's sails to dry whilst they mend nets and brim the hull as one man can be seen doing. There was obviously a good breeze that day as the telling movement of the mizzen and main sails show.*

**PZ11**
Oil and pencil on card 7¼ x 11 in (18.2 x 28 cm) Image courtesy of Sotheby's

**Three Luggers**
Oil and pencil on card 7 x 18 in (17.8 x 45.7 cm) Portland Gallery

*19th century photograph of St Ives mackerel boats.*
Photo: St Ives Archive

**Fishing Lugger**
Image courtesy of Sotheby's

**Fishing Boat and Lighthouse**
Private Collection

**Black Boat and Grey Sea**

Private Collection

*PZ484, 2nd class lugger named* Bessie *from Newlyn.*

**Sail**

Private Collection

*SS10, a 1st class lugger named* Uncle Tom *with a crew of six men and one boy. The boat fished from St Ives 1883 -1911. Verso of painting* Steam, *p56.*

*Fishing lugger, St Ives Harbour.*
Photo: St Ives Archive

**Boat in Harbour, Red Sail Mainmast Unstepped**
Oil on card 7 x 18¼ in (18 x 46.5 cm) Kettle's Yard, University of Cambridge

*Fish landing on Newlyn old harbour.*

Photo: St Ives Archive

*The old quay at Newlyn was built in the 1400s and was later enclosed by the much larger quays built in the nineteenth century. The Newlyn and Penzance fleet would anchor off during the day in an area of water known as Gwavas Lake, as is shown in Stanhope Forbes's well-known painting* A Fish Sale on a Cornish Beach.

**Fishing Boats Anchored by Pier and Lighthouse**
Oil and pencil on card 4¼ x 8⅞ in (10.8 x 22.5 cm)
Kettle's Yard, University of Cambridge

*The routine for most of the fishing fleet was to leave port in the late afternoon, and to arrive on the fishing grounds to shoot their nets at dusk, hauling the nets at dawn and returning to harbour in the morning. After landing the fish, in fine weather the boats were often left outside the harbour at anchor, where, whatever the tide, they were always afloat, ready for the next night's fishing. The mainsail was taken down and the mast stepped to reduce rolling in the swells. Even today, if you visit St Ives in the summer you will see boats anchored off the harbour.*

**Two Fishermen in their Ship One Mast Stepped**
Oil on card 7½ x 9 in (19 x 22.9 cm)
Kettle's Yard, University of Cambridge

# St Ives

## The Marine Stores
## Old Iron

St Ives harbour was a busy place in the latter part of the nineteenth century. The fishing industry was thriving at the time and the railway arrived there in 1877, allowing fish, packed in ice, to be sent to the rest of the country. In the 1880s, fishing in St Ives was at its zenith with many mackerel and pilchard boats working from the harbour. Although by that time local tin and copper mines were in decline, sail and steamships still brought in Welsh coal for the pumping engines, carrying out tin and copper ore to be smelted in Wales. Each year, ships stocked with barrels of pilchards from the many pilchard cellars in St Ives made regular voyages to Italy and Spain.

In late summer, the seine fishery boats that had been laid up all year at the top of Porthminster Beach were launched. In those days, hundreds of tons of pilchards were caught in the late summer and autumn. There was a local saying that the wealth of St Ives was built on pilchards and mining, and another that all the wealth in the town passed through the harbour gap.

In the 1860s, a wooden pier, known as the 'New Pier', was built to the seaward side of Smeaton's Pier to accommodate the growing number of boats in the fishing fleet. Wooden structures do not last in Atlantic gales, and after about twenty years the pier was destroyed by the sea. Its remains can still be seen at low tide. During the 1890s the people of St Ives saw the extension of Smeaton's Pier and the construction of a new lighthouse. The three arches at the top end of the pier were added to help clear sand from the harbour.

The town of St Ives is divided into two parts. Downalong, with its narrow maze of cobbled streets, is the lower and oldest part of the town, where the fishermen lived in the granite and whitewashed cottages that crowd around the harbour. There were many shops and pubs in the town; the Sloop Inn dates to 1322. Upalong, on higher ground, was inhabited by the miners, tradesmen, incomers and the more affluent. They lived in terraced rows of Victorian houses stretching back up the hill and away from the fishing village.

It is said that the people of St Ives are particularly bright, as for generations, through necessity, their diet was rich in fish. Ray were known as 'upstairs (to the bedroom) fish' and consuming them was believed to produce boys. This close-knit community would experience great poverty if the fishing failed. Perhaps as a result of hardship, like many fishing communities that have experienced the fragility of life and suffered lives lost at sea, these people with their distinctive, sing-song Cornish accent, had a philosophical attitude and a strong sense of humour.

*Ready to Launch, St. Ives, 1880-1885.*
Photo: St Ives Museum
*Many sailing ships and fishing boats were built in the harbour in the nineteenth century.*

*St Ives Harbour, 19th century.*

Photo: St Ives Museum

*A fine day in St Ives. Outside the harbour the fishing fleet heads to sea, while lines of washing are put out to dry on the strand. Above, on the quay is St Leonard's Chapel and the harbourmaster's office and to the right of that, the hand-powered crane that was used to move the baulks of timber in the arches below; this controlled the amount of sand in the harbour. This crane can be dated from the 1890s to the 1920s. The timbers at the wooden jetty, which feature in many of Wallis's paintings of the harbour are visible beyond the harbour wall. Centre: a schooner lies on its moorings, sails set - about to sail, just arrived or just drying sails.*

*19th century glass plate photographs.*
Photo: Private Collection
*Fishing fleet drying sails in St Ives Harbour.*

*19th century glass plate photographs.*
Photo: Private Collection
*Fishing boats St Ives Harbour.*

Charles Wallis ran the Marine Stores in Albert Street near the harbour in Penzance, dealing in second-hand marine gear and scrap metal. The business was owned by Joe Denley, who was evidently an entrepreneurial character as he also traded in corn, coal and general merchandise.

Berlin described Joe Denley as 'a hard businessman. Short in stature and shabby in appearance. He wore the same clothes "Sundays and Mondays". On a Sunday morning he would be found on the harbour looking "as miserable as sin", his long unkempt hair hanging down over a dirty collar. It is said that he died leaving £500,000.'

It is thought that Alfred Wallis helped his brother in the Marine Stores business during periods when he was not at sea, as it seems Joe Denley asked him to set up a similar operation in St Ives. Sometime in the mid-1880s, Alfred and Susan Wallis left Penzance and moved to St Ives. Peter Barnes has traced them to premises in Back Road in 1887. St Ives Museum holds a number of nineteenth-century poor rate registers. The record for 7 April 1898 shows that Wallis had moved to the premises on the wharf. The six-monthly register notes that he paid eleven shillings and threepence in rates for the house and cellar.

*But it was not long before they moved to No. 4, Bethesda Hill, a steep, narrow alley running up behind the western end of the harbour. It was here the business got well founded and Wallis became a part of the town and its life. The new home was a four-roomed cottage of brown granite with steps and a twisted iron rail running up to the front door, next to which there was a large cellar where he carried on his business.*[14]

Clearly painted on the cellar door of the building on the wharf overlooking the harbour was:
'A WALLIS DEALER IN MARINE STORES'. (letter 'N' inverted)

It is worth remembering the important part religion played in society in those days; several religious denominations flourished in St Ives. Many of the St Ives fishermen were highly religious, and would not go to sea on the sabbath. Indeed, in St Ives Sunday-keeping was a tradition rigorously observed by all and upheld until the 1980s, though the influence of religion has clearly diminished over time.

The founder of the Salvation Army, William Booth, came to St Ives in 1862 to teach the Bible, and he had a large following. One of the sights on a summer's evening in St Ives was the Salvation Army band marching around the harbour, playing and holding services in the open air. Susan Wallis had been a member of the Salvation Army since their Penzance days, and in St Ives she was a Sunday-school teacher. Alfred Wallis, signed the 'Articles of War', joining the Salvation Army in 1904. Both Alfred and Susan held strong religious beliefs throughout their lives.

*Marine Stores with donkey, etc.*
Photo: St Ives Museum
*A gathering of chattering women in starched aprons stands in front of Wallis's Marine Stores. Wallis's donkey and cart on the right. After 1898.*

*The wharf in St Ives.*
Photo: St Ives Museum
*Wallis, with bowler hat, is standing in the boat.*

*Outside the Marine Stores on the harbour front, before 1912.*
Photo: St Ives Museum

*Wallis's pony and cart loaded with household items. Clearly, Wallis's business traded in more than marine scrap, see the cane chairs and linoleum on the cart. The cellar door, painted 'A WALLIS DEALER IN MARINE STORES', is placed against the brickwork of the building.*

*Alfred Wallis, c1890.*
Photo: St Ives Archive

**An Industrious Man**

What picture of Wallis can we draw during his period in the Marine Stores? The fishing industry generated a variety of marine items to be bought and sold, including metal fittings, chains, sails and rope that came from the boats. Wallis travelled the streets of St Ives with his donkey and cart, collecting scrap, and Joe Denley sent wagons to St Ives to take Wallis's collections back to Penzance. Photographs showing the front of his store clearly indicate that he dealt in all sorts of goods. His call earned him the nickname 'Old Iron'. With the presence of the Marine Stores on the harbour front, Alfred and Susan Wallis became an accepted part of the St Ives community.

Berlin recounts that Wallis kept the donkey clean and groomed and treated him well, but the donkey's braying at night disturbed the neighbours. When the donkey died Wallis walked to Devon to buy a Dartmoor pony, which he used to pull a cart laden with his collection of scrap to Penzance. He would not ride on the cart, but walked alongside the pony. A number of Wallis's paintings were evidently inspired by the landscape he knew from his journeys across west Penwith.

Alfred and Susan Wallis were a hard-working couple who were willing to turn their hand to whatever was necessary to earn a living. Ice was used in the fishing industry and so was readily available; with his youngest step-son, Jacob Ward, Wallis made and sold ice-cream. They were the first in St Ives to do this, and people remarked that their ice-cream was pink.

Wallis had a pet duck and kept chickens in his back yard:

*His next door neighbour, Mr Lander, also kept fowls. Among Lander's birds there was a big rooster who was always coming over the wall and fighting with Alfred's rooster. This was annoying Wallis, but instead of saying anything about it he wrote to his old friend and step-son George Ward, explaining the circumstances and asking for an English Fighting Cock to be sent. George at that time was farming in Okehampton. In the course of time a huge fighting cock, bred in the true English tradition arrived at Bethesda Hill. Alfred took it out the back, put it in a hutch and waited. When Lander's rooster first appeared on the wall he let the cock out.* [15]

Mr Lander's bird was killed. *'And with the first thrust of's great spurs 'e kill'd un!'* to quote Mr and Mrs Ward.

Dr Slack's interviews with local people who knew Wallis indicate that he was remembered as a good businessman who worked hard and, at that time seems to have been in a position to lend money.

*Figures on the wharf.*
Photo: St Ives Museum
*The Marine Stores on the left 1907.*

*Steps and alleyway at the side of Marine Stores.*
Photo: St Ives Museum
*Susan Wallis on the upper right in doorway.*

Charles Wallis continued to live in Penzance until 4th January 1908, when he died of tuberculosis. Alfred Wallis hired two large cars to take members of his and Susan's family to Penzance for the funeral. Later that year, on 1st August, Wallis paid Mr Daniel Hollow £93 for a cottage, No. 3 Back Road West, St Ives.

Quotes from Dr Slack's interviews:

### Jacob Ward:

*He was known to be straight in his dealings. If he said tuppence, he meant tuppence. Sometimes boys would pinch items from him and try to sell them to him again. Boys who stole from him could never have any more to do with Alfred Wallis.*

### Jessie Farrell

*He had a good business on the wharf, see. I can see my Granny down there now sorting out the stuff. The cottons from the woollens, they used to make paper from that. I can remember the little pony he had, Albert he was called.*

### Thomas Lander

*What I mean to say was, he was an industrious man, he was never poor. Never poor.*

It has been generally accepted that Wallis started painting in 1925, but these and similar statements provide evidence that he made drawings far earlier than this, which suggests he had always been creative and interested in expressing himself visually.

### Jacob Ward:

*No, he started to paint - well yes - I mean to say he'd do a lot of painting and Grandma used to laugh at him, when he had the Marine Stores. Yes, he painted then, I was very silly really you know, 'cause I could have got different paintings of his, but used to laugh at them we did as children. He used to do quite a bit of sketching when he had the Marine Stores, that's lots of years ago when I was eight years old.*

### Dr Slack:

*But this is a great surprise, because I don't think anyone knew this.*

### Jacob Ward:

*Oh yes, I know I did, because I've gone out there and Grandma used to be sitting beside the old grate there, and Grandfather used to have a bit of old paper. But yes, he done a bit of drawing before he ever started to paint. Yes, I know that, I don't know what became of his stuff. I suppose, like everything else, a lot of it was burnt you know.*

Quote from a recording in St Ives Archive:

### Harry Richards

*Alfred would get cigarette packets to draw on from children who would pick them up for him.*

When he started painting Wallis remembered features of the landscape of West Penwith he would have known well and seen when he made his regular journeys from St Ives to Penzance with his collection of scrap.

**Picking Flowers**
Oil on card 8¼ x 18½ in (21 x 47 cm) Image courtesy of Sotheby's
*In spring, daffodil pickers working in the fields of west Cornwall are still a common sight to this day.*

**Cottages in a wood, St Ives**
Oil on card 11½ x 18¾ in (29.5 x 47.5 cm) Kettle's Yard, University of Cambridge

**Landscape with two large Trees and Houses**
Oil on card 11¾ x 9 in (29.8 x 22.8 cm)
Kettle's Yard, University of Cambridge

*Trees, houses and gardens are recurring theme in Wallis's work. The following paintings evoke houses and trees seen from the coastal path walk from St Ives to Carbis Bay.*

### Farmland and Animals

Oil on card 12½ x 19½ in (31.7 x 49.5 cm) Private Collection

*This painting is particularly reminiscent of the coastal landscape seen from the roads of west Penwith where the ancient stone-wall fields lead down to the cliff edge with the sea beyond, a landscape that, to this day, has changed little. From here, as in Wallis's day, passing shipping can still be seen.*

### Knill's Monument

Oil and pencil on card 6¾ x 8¼ in (17 x 21 cm) Kettle's Yard, University of Cambridge

*Near St Ives, on Worvas Hill, stands Knill's Monument, a 50-foot-high granite obelisk erected by John Knill, one-time mayor of St Ives. He prescribed an elaborate ceremony that was to take place every five years around the monument. It involved ten young dancing girls from the families of fishermen, dressed in white, two widows in black, and a fiddler to play the 'Furry Dance'. This folk ceremony is still enacted every five years, making the monument the centrepiece of a unique living tradition.*

*Above: Knill's Monument.*
Photo: Royal Cornwall Museum

**Cornish Landscape with Cows**

Oil and pencil on card laid on panel 6 x 14 in (15 x 35.6 cm) Image courtesy of Sotheby's

*On his walks to St Ives, Wallis would have passed the mine workings of Consul's Mine and those on Rosewall Hill.*

*Mine workings Rosewall Hill, and in the distance Consul's Mines and St Ives.*

*Salvation Army Corps.*

Photo: St Ives Museum

*Front row: Wallis in bowler hat, sitting, third from right.*

*Above: Alfred Wallis, detail from previous photograph.*
Photo: St Ives Museum

*Left: Salvation Army Articles of War; signed by Alfred Wallis, March 1904.*

**SS *Rosedale***

During his period in the Marine Stores, an incident occurred that must have caused Wallis some embarrassment. On 17th November 1893, several ships were taking shelter from a south-easterly gale in St Ives Bay. During the night, the wind veered to the north-east and increased to storm force. Three sailing ships, *Cintra, Vulture* and *Bessie*, all carrying coal, were wrecked and driven ashore in Carbis Bay.

The next day the storm continued, and the steel steamship *Rosedale*, 'in ballast' from Southampton to Cardiff, also found herself in difficulties off the coast. In an attempt to save the vessel, the captain brought the ship in to St Ives Bay, and ran her ashore on Porthminster Beach. The St Ives lifeboat was launched and also got into difficulties. With six oars smashed, the lifeboat was washed up on the beach near SS *Rosedale*; thankfully, all the crew members from both vessels survived.

It was hoped that SS *Rosedale* could be refloated, but the ship started to break up and this proved impossible. During the next few weeks, a considerable amount of looting from the wreck took place. Two young men, James Stevens and Richard Taylor, had taken some brass bands from the anchor winch, and these ended up in Wallis's possession. He was arrested while taking them to Denley in Penzance. In January 1894, he appeared in court in St Ives charged with receiving stolen goods, and he paid a fine of £10, avoiding a two-month prison sentence. Unable to pay their 25 shilling fines, the young men each spent one month in Bodmin Gaol. Eventually, SS *Rosedale* had to be dismantled with explosives; reports describe pieces of metal falling over a wide area, including the town of St Ives.

*SS* Rosedale.
Photo: St Ives Archive
*The seine boats are in the foreground.*

*SS* Rosedale *aground off Porthminster Beach.*
Photos: St Ives Archive

*Above: St Ives Harbour 19th century.*
Photo: St Ives Museum, St Ives Archive

*One of the large iron buoys is seen here between the masts of the boat in the middle distance. In the left foreground a punt is being skulled with a single oar at the stern. Wallis features a punt being skulled in* This is Sein Fishery That Used To Be *on page 209.*

*Right: Schooner in St Ives harbour at low tide with large iron bouys.*
Photo: St Ives Archive

**Boats Near the Harbour**

Oil and pencil on card 7¼ x 11⅝ in (18.5 x 29.5 cm) Belgrave Gallery, St Ives

*Two steamships and two luggers approach St. Ives harbour. On the left of the painting Wallis remembers one of the large iron buoys that was used for warping vessels into St. Ives harbour.*

**Money Matters**

The Marine Stores lasted for twenty two years. Susan, an important figure in the business, was growing old; in 1912 she was seventy-seven and Alfred was fifty-six. When the business ceased they were living at 3, Back Road West, St Ives, the cottage they had purchased from Mr Hollow in 1908.

During the First World War, Wallis helped to make huts for the government on the Island in St Ives. At times, he did odd jobs such as moving furniture for his friend Mr Armour who had an antique shop in Fore Street.

*Active? 'e'd move furniture like a boy. And walk! walk Penzance! I can see en now - allies 'ad 'is trousers too big; 'e didn't care; rolled the buggers up; a fisherman's jersey and an ole cap. goin' along the road there with my handcart. I couldn't catch't en up. Deaf an' all - 'e couldn't hear me shouten. One day I chased en all the way to Carbis Bay!* [16]

Although by this time Susan Wallis was in receipt of a pension, it seems that the couple were not doing well financially. In 1915, Wallis was summoned to appear at the town hall for arrears in 'poor rates' amounting to the sum of £5/6d.

Susan died on 7th June 1922 at the age of eighty-eight. The funeral was conducted by the Salvation Army.

At the end of Susan's life an incident occurred that caused Alfred Wallis considerable distress. As Berlin describes:

*In the bedroom of their cottage Susan and Alfred kept an old trunk in which clean and best bedlinen was stored. Along with this linen was the sum of £40 in gold and £5 in silver. During Susan's last illness, the children then living were constant visitors. Their mother was growing weaker each day, and 'a bit light in the 'ead'. After her death Alfred went to the trunk to find out his financial position only to discover that the money was gone and all the bedlinen and blankets changed for old ones. It was generally thought that Albert Ward was the culprit. Each week when he took the laundry home he had exchanged the bedclothes, and on returning them to the trunk had helped himself to the money until it was gone. Albert died in 1928 aged 65.*

*According to another report Alfred did not say who took the money. He simply said 'All I know, it wasn't there afterwards!'*

*It was after Susan's death that Alfred Wallis turned on the Wards, saying he wished he'd never met the family. Apparently he was under the illusion that there was quite a lot of money saved against his old age, but it turned out that Susan had been continually helping her children through difficulties, and although it is said that in earlier years Alfred had always shown himself to be of assistance to them, he nursed a strong grudge about it later, just as he had done with his brother Charles. The resentment grew as time went on. He refused point blank to have anything to do with them.*

*Fortunately there had been a little money in the Post Office on which he was able to live for a short time after Susan's death. When this was exhausted he mortgaged his cottage to a Mr. Spinks for £50. This was arranged by Mr. Armour senior who was one of those who saw Wallis's first paintings and encouraged him to go on. Mr. Spinks later sold the cottage to Mr. Care of St Ives, on condition that Care did not take over until Wallis was dead.*

William Care lived a few doors up the road from Wallis in a red brick house called The Doll's House. For many years, his son John Care was the fiddler at the Knill's Monument ceremony.

# Starting to Paint

**St Ives Artist Colony**

The extension of the railway to Penzance and St Ives had a significant effect on the region's economy and brought major social change. More people came to the area and the summer tourist industry grew. Artists came and settled, some of whom had been working in Brittany; for them, life in these remote Cornish fishing communities, where the local people spoke in a strong Cornish dialect, must have been almost like being abroad.

Newlyn's art colony was developing while Wallis was fishing from there, and by the turn of the century there was a well-established artist community in St Ives. As the fishing industry went into decline, fishermen's net lofts became artists' studios.

The work of the artists of Newlyn and St Ives was being exhibited in London, and each year until the First World War a special railway carriage took their pictures to the Royal Academy. One of the year's big events was Open Day, when artists invited the public to visit their studios. On the whole, the work of the St Ives artists was representational, atmospheric and based on observation, and it was mainly concerned with landscape and seascape. Painters were a common sight working at their easels outside in the *en plein air* tradition.

**Houses at St Ives, Cornwall**
Oil on card 10½ x 12½ in (26.7 x 31.8 cm) Tate, London 2001

St Ives

Oil on card 10 x 15¼ in (25.7 x 38.4 cm) Tate, London 2001

*Norway Cottage, St Ives.*

**Street Corner**
Oil on card 6 x 8¾ in (15 x 22 cm) Private Collection
*Norway Cottage centre, and a cottage in Porthmeor Square on the right. On the left of the painting Back Road West and the row of cottages where Alfred Wallis lived at number 3. At the top is The Doll's House, where Mr Care lived. In the latter part of Wallis's life Mr Care bought his cottage but allowed Wallis to remain there until his death.*

### Starting to Paint

In the years following Susan's death Wallis began to paint - 'for company' he said. The presence of so many artists in the area could have influenced Wallis's decision to do 'a bit of paintin'. Perhaps this was also an expression of his entrepreneurial spirit. As Dr Slack's tape recordings reveal, Wallis had been making drawings during his time at the Marine Stores. Now he called on his memories of his seagoing years, to paint the ships and fishing boats he had seen and worked aboard. He painted the harbours and coasts he knew from both land and sea, and the areas of Penwith he was familiar with. He depicted the town of St Ives as he knew and remembered it. During the period he had been in St Ives, the copper and tin mines in the area had closed, and the pilchards no longer came, the fishing industry had declined and the seine fishery had ceased working.

His paintings depict a wide variety of places and events. He recalled lighthouses, harbours, buoys, buildings in towns and details of landscape, woods, bridges, animals and birds. He had seen shipwrecks and the flights of early aeroplanes and balloons, and they all found their way into his paintings. He reminisced about a way of life which, by the time he started to paint, had virtually disappeared.

Wallis painted on anything he could get hold of: pieces of cardboard, bits of wood, tin lids, discarded calendars, old envelopes, jars, cups, plates, and even furniture and parts of his house. George Farrell, who remembered Wallis, commented that with Wallis 'nothing was safe from where paint could go'.

Cardboard was Wallis's favourite material, which was often supplied by his friend Mr Baughan who kept a grocer's shop in St Ives. The pieces of cardboard were frequently irregular in shape, which Wallis would often 'improve' with scissors. The odd shapes of his paintings became a feature of his work, and by making his compositions fit the shapes of the boards he demonstrated his intuitive and original sense of design. In some paintings, one can see that the shape of the board has determined the layout of the painting. One feels a rightness in his work and, at times, a sense of surprise and wit. He often worked into the painting with pencil. Sometimes his work has been thickly painted, but often parts are left unpainted, allowing the colour of the board to become an integral part of the picture. He constantly reminds us of the materials he uses and the surface on which he is working.

The sort of paint he used was important to Wallis. He did not want artist's oil paint, but preferred household paint and liked a specific brand of enamel favoured by fishermen for the coloured parts of their boats. It cost sixpence a tin from Mr Burrell's shop in the Digey. His favourite colours were white, grey, black, brown, blue and what Nicholson refers to as 'a particularly pungent Cornish Green'. It would be easy to assume that his limited palette was due to short supply but this may not be the case - note Wallis's remark: 'Been a lot of paintings spoiled By putin Collers where They do not Belong'.

The Hold House, Porthmeor Square Island Porthmeor Beach
Oil on card 12 x 15¼ in (30.5 x 38.5 cm) Tate

**Houses Porthmeor Square**
Oil and pencil on card 5½ × 10½ in (14 x 26.7 cm)
Courtesy of Sotheby's

*This painting shows Norway Cottage, Porthmeor Square and nearby cottages. Wallis made many paintings of the subject. On the left of the painting, Back Road West and the row of cottages where Wallis lived at number 3 is depicted from a different angle, another example of Wallis working from multiple viewpoints.*

**Bill Wallis:**
Bill Wallis, the grandson of Alfred Wallis's brother Charles, remembers his Great Uncle Alfred
*'scurrying down Fore Street with a collection of cardboard scraps under his arm'.*
(From an interview I made with Bill Wallis in 2006 see page 225)

**Elizabeth Lewis**
I met 94-year-old Elizabeth Lewis in 2011. She was born in 1917 and lived in Porthmeor Square till she was ten years old, when the family moved to another part of St Ives. She had clear memories of Wallis from her childhood. She and her friend Mary would play in the square and would often see the artist through his open door. The following comes from our conversation, recorded in 2011.

*Mr Wallis lived round the corner from me. He lived in a small cottage. He was a very small man and a very pleasant man.*

*He would sit inside, and used to play a music box, a concertina thing. He would sit there with the door open.*

*On the wall, when we looked inside, were all these paintings of ships. Some were going up a wave, some used to go on top of the wave. He would paint on anything. He painted on the cupboard, he painted on bits of cardboard. He couldn't afford to buy artists materials. Sometimes he would give them to friends. Sometimes they threw them away. They thought he was crazy. The ships would go any way, all put on the wall in his kitchen. When he died, someone had the key to his house. They called in the artist people. They were very kind, these artist people. They paid for everything. He was buried in a grave three away from my parents.*

**Sailing ships, steamers and fish**
Oil on wooden panels 27 x 27 in (58.5 x 68.5 cm) Private Collection
*Wall panel. A section of the painted wooden panelling (wainscotting) from Alfred Wallis's cottage at No. 3 Back Road West.*

*George Farrell:*
'He used to have a passion for painting mackerel boats, you know, mackerel luggers, double end mackerel luggers, and they used to be used to make a frieze of them all along the wainscotting'.

*He went in the big boats, I think he painted what he remembered ... The walls were covered in paintings. Mr Care bought the house ... Mr Care used to own Porthmeor Beach and Porthgwidden Beach. He also bought the Doll's House and lived there.*

*He must have painted with ordinary paint. He could not afford to buy artist's paints. He lived on his own. If he saw a bit of cardboard he would paint on it. By the time I was born his wife was gone. The wall was covered, absolutely covered. Everything was covered up with ships. Really lovely ships. He painted very well.*

*He was a very pleasant-looking man, with a moustache, grey of course. There were other artists in the town at the time. We would stand behind them and have a look. We knew quite a lot of those artist people.*

*In the night, fishermen were out catching herring. When they were coming in, mother would go down in the morning to count up the fish.*

Elizabeth Lewis's recollections of Alfred sitting down playing an instrument on his lap substantiate Berlin's description of Susan's long association with the Salvation Army:

*Susan, on the other hand, was such an energetic worker for the Salvationist cause, among her fellow men, that for many years after her death she was remembered for her cottage meetings.*

*It is in connection with these meetings that I have traced the first link with a portable organ, or 'melodeon,' which Alfred used to play to himself as an old man after Susan's death. It was originally used for these meetings conducted by Susan in the cottages of the fisherman, but whether it was Alfred who actually played on these occasions I have been unable to find out.*

*He had one friend at the time named Mark Hollow. Hollow was a very religious man. He used to visit Alfred frequently. They spent their time reading the Bible, talking and singing hymns to the old 'melodeon', which Alfred played. But Hollow died.*

*It was a curious instrument. The performer sat on a chair with the organ on his knees, operating the bellows with his left hand at the back and playing with his right. That helped to drive him to hold his own service alone in his cottage, playing the organ, from which, Mr Edwards tells us, 'He could whack out a good tune.'*

Terry Stevens grew up in St Ives. His parents ran the Willow Pattern Tearooms in Digey Square, and as a boy he played in the area close to where Wallis lived. I met him in 2004 and he recalled how he and his friends would go into the artist's house, where, painted on the pine-topped kitchen table, was a picture of St Ives Bay, and on the door to the kitchen was a portrait of Susan Wallis. The boys did not think much of Wallis's paintings, believing they could do as well themselves. He remembers that Scottish women and those from fishing ports in the northeast used to come every year to pack the fish. They followed the fleet, staying in lodgings in the town. Despite the fact that their dialect was so strong that he could not understand much of what was being said, he did recall that the swearing was terrible.

*Left:* **Old Arch Digey** (inscribed with title)
Oil on card 4¼ x 3 in (11 x 7.8 cm) Private Collection

*Right: The old arch, St Ives.*
Photo: St Ives Archive

### Irene Lander

I met Irene Lander In 2018. She grew up in St Ives where she was born. Her family lived at No 4 Back Road West, not far from Alfred Wallis, but on the other side of the road, opposite Porthmeor Studios. As children Irene and her friends played on the steps of the studios and saw many of the artists coming and going. She remarked that in those days artists painting outside in St Ives were 'a common sight'.

She particularly remembered the portrait painter Leonard Fuller. Irene had clear memories of Alfred Wallis, describing him as 'a quiet gentleman'. She had not gone into his house, but remembered seeing paintings 'all over the walls' through the open door.

Sometimes Wallis gave her paintings 'to take home for the family'. Like many others she and her family considered these offerings child-like, and her mother instructed her to 'chuck them away'. Irene recollected being given at least 12 postcard-sized paintings over the years, which had all been thrown away or burnt.

# Finding Wallis

While visiting Cornwall in the summer of 1928, Ben and Winifred Nicholson and Christopher Wood were staying in cottages that belonged to Marcus and Irene Brumwell's family at Pill Creek near Truro. John Wells was also staying nearby. On a day trip to St Ives, Ben Nicholson and Christopher Wood came across Alfred Wallis looking, as Wood claimed, 'just like Cézanne'.

The story of this event is best told in Ben Nicholson's own words:

*In August 1928 I went over for the day to St Ives with Kit Wood; this was an exciting day, for not only was it the first time I saw St Ives, but on the way from Porthmeor beach we passed an open back door in Back Road West, and through it I saw some paintings of ships and houses on odd pieces of paper and cardboard nailed up all over the wall, with particularly large nails through the smallest ones. We knocked on the door and inside found Wallis, and the paintings we got from him then were the first he made.* [17]

In his paintings, they recognised something new. Ben Nicholson described Wallis's paintings as 'a truthful, fresh way of conveying reality'.

Here was *'An art, simple, direct, honest ... unencumbered by theory, completely true to itself'*. [18]

### Schooner and Lighthouse

Oil on card 6½ x 12 in (16.5 x 30.5 cm) Private Collection
c. 1925-8.
*Ben Nicholson bought this painting from Alfred Wallis for two shillings and sixpence when they first met at 3 Back Road West in 1928.*

*Alfred Wallis and Ben Nicholson.*
Photo: Private Collection

*So he leads his life, puffing his pipe, reading his bible, and improvising strange melodies on a kind of strange organ he has and painting memories of the past on the backs and sides of cardboard boxes which he gets from a neighbouring grocer.* [19]

*Certainly his vision is a remarkable thing with an intensity and depth of experience which makes it much more than merely child-like.* [20]

Wallis must have been greatly encouraged by the interest that Nicholson and Wood showed in his work. Nicholson goes on to say that

*He was a very fierce and lonely little man, and I think it obviously meant a great deal to him (almost everything in fact, as it does to any artist) to have the idea in his painting appreciated and taken seriously.*

Nicholson also recalled that

*the neighbourhood where he lived regard him as an eccentric curiosity, and his paintings as nothing at all.*

Kindly neighbours sent their children to Wallis with meals, and he would give them paintings to take home in return. Dr Slack interviewed some of these children, now adults, who said that their parents thought so little of these offerings that they threw them away or used them to light the fire. Similarly, at the baker's shop where Wallis bought his bread, they did not know what to do with all the paintings he had given them so they burnt them in the oven. Another shopkeeper commented that 'We would always wait till he'd left the shop before we put his paintings in the bin', and a neighbour who was given a painting used it to stop the draught coming down the chimney.

It would appear that many of the other artists in St Ives saw little value in Wallis's work. It probably seemed to them as childish and silly as it did to most of the people in Wallis's life.

*The fact that Wallis's cottage was almost next door to the St Ives Society of Artists is worth comment for the oddly irrational situation it presents. These artists did not consider him anything but a crazy old man who wasted his time creating rubbish.* [21]

*Alfred Wallis in the doorway of his cottage,
3 Back Road West, St Ives.*
Photo: Private Collection

*Alfred Wallis (Photographs by Ben Nicholson) 1928.*
Photos: Private Collection

*Alfred Wallis's letter to Ben Nicholson.*
The Winifred Nicholson Archive

That summer, Ben and Winifred Nicholson came to stay in St Ives for three weeks, renting a flat overlooking the harbour.

Wood went on to lodge in a cottage overlooking Porthmeor Beach, St Ives, for three months, and during this time visited Wallis regularly. He wrote to Nicholson: 'Admiral Wallis I often see' and 'more and more influence de Wallis, not a bad master though'. Wood returned to Cornwall once more in 1930, spending three weeks in Mousehole, before he met his death under a train at Salisbury station. Presumably Nicholson had told Wallis of Wood's death, as in a letter dated November 1930, Wallis mentions the difficulty of sending large paintings, and also refers to the death of Wood ('you must feel it very much it is a heavy Blaw').

*November 1930*

*Sir i Racevied your cheque all Right and am glad they peased about The Big pictures ply wood Boxes would not long a month for 2 of them so I must Try and get a small Case for Them. You said aBout a picture of mr wood i should like to have someThiss what he have don himself you must feel it very much it is a heavy Blaw I got som here and i have Tried The harbour That was on The p st Card and The Boats i will send it on with The nex parcle so I must for The Time Best Respects To all oping you are all well and opin mrs wood is getting over hir sad Brevement*

*From your True friend alfred wallis*

Nicholson kept in touch with Wallis during the 1930s, mainly by correspondence when buying Wallis's paintings. From the bundles of paintings Wallis sent him, he built up a large collection and later gave many away to friends. Wallis also made a model fishing boat (a St Ives lugger) for the Nicholson family.

Ben and Winifred Nicholson were members of the Seven and Five Society, and exhibited two examples of Wallis's work alongside theirs at the Tooth Gallery, London in 1929. In 1931, Wallis's paintings were hung in an exhibition in the Lucy Carrington Wertheim Gallery. In 1940 Ben Nicholson gave one of Wallis's paintings (*St Ives Harbour,* c.1932-3) to the Museum of Modern Art in New York.

The Nicholsons also introduced Wallis's work to other buyers, including Adrian Stokes and his wife Margaret Mellis and also Barbara Hepworth, Herbert Read and H.S. Ede, who was then an assistant at the Tate Gallery in London. Ede never met the artist, but like Nicholson received bundles of paintings from Wallis, some of which he sent back along with a cheque for the ones he wanted to keep. The paintings he bought then form the large collection of Wallis's work held at Kettle's Yard, Cambridge.

In 1931, Ben and Winifred Nicholson separated. At the outbreak of war in 1939, Nicholson, who was now married to Barbara Hepworth, came to St Ives again - initially staying at Little Parc Owles, Carbis Bay, the home of Adrian Stokes and Margaret Mellis.

Others who bought or took interest in his work were Peter Lanyon, Bernard Leach and Miriam Gabo, the wife of the Russian Constructivist sculptor Naum Gabo (they too came to St Ives in 1939 at the invitation of Stokes and Mellis). Edwin Mullins estimated that 'in all there cannot have been more than one or two dozen people who took an interest in Wallis's work during his lifetime'.

*Jake Nicholson with a boat given by Alfred Wallis, Cornwall, 1932*
Photo: Private Collection

**Schooner in full sail near a lighthouse**
Oil on card 9¾ x 20 in (24.5 x 51 cm) Kettle's Yard, University of Cambridge

*Photograph of the Christopher Wood painting* Market Cross Tréboul *1930.*
Private Collection

**Mary Waters, St Ives**
Oil on card 5⅞ x 7 in (14.8 x 17.8 cm) Private Collection

Mary Waters *was owned in St Ives and could often be seen in the harbour. Although Wallis has inscribed 'Mary Waters St Ives' on the painting, it is unlikely that he sailed aboard the ship. This painting was made in 1929. Ships articles show that* Mary Waters *was involved in the home and European trade and visited the Mediterranean.*

Ben or Winifred Nicholson sent Wallis this photograph of Christopher Wood's work; Wallis painted on the reverse and sent it back.

Right:
**Christopher Wood, Ships and Lighthouse Cornwall**
(Also known as Harbour in the Hills) 1928
Oil on canvas 14 x 17 in (36 x 43.6cm)
Courtesy of University of Essex

Below:
**Christopher Wood, PZ134** 1930
Oil on board 19½ x 27¼ in (50 x 69.2cm)
The Lucy Carrington Wertheim Bequest. Towner Eastbourne

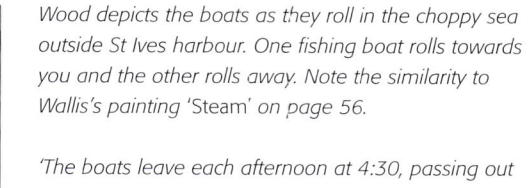

*Wood depicts the boats as they roll in the choppy sea outside St Ives harbour. One fishing boat rolls towards you and the other rolls away. Note the similarity to Wallis's painting 'Steam' on page 56.*

*'The boats leave each afternoon at 4:30, passing out within 5 yards of the lighthouse so one can see them well. They stay out in this dreadful weather till 9 then come in and go out again at 10 till 5 & 6 in the morning, they then look after their nets and as they say but the time they have had a cup tea and a smoke it's time to start off again. No sleep on this blasted job, they say'.* [22]

*'Wood was still experimenting and his St Ives pictures are at their best when responding to Wallis. His palette became similar to Wallis's and he painted 'mostly in black, white, grey, dark blue and brown.'* [23]

**Winifred Nicholson, Boat on a Stormy Sea** 1928.

Oil on canvas 21½ x 31½ in (55 x 80 cm) Private Collection

*'Winifred's response to Wallis's imagination was the most straightforward of the three artists.* Boat on a Stormy Sea *has a new-found freedom; you sense her delight in conjuring a storm with one long swish of her paint-laden brush, the spray thrown high in the air by the rocks, and the fishing boat has the movement of a Wallis boat.'* **24**

Wallis's work had a significant influence on Ben and Winifred Nicholson and Christopher Wood. Ideas embodied in the paintings of this untutored old man coincided with current artistic concerns and, in turn, his work helped to shape and develop those ideas. They were searching for a simple and direct way of expressing themselves, and clearly identified with the naive qualities they saw in Wallis's paintings. For them Wallis appears to have acted as a liberating force. After three months in St Ives, Wood went to Brittany. The paintings he made in Brittany in 1929 and Cornwall in 1928 and 1930 have been recognised as his finest work.

Among the few people that valued his work at the time of its production was a group of artists who would become important figures in the art of St Ives and the Modern Movement.

Ben Nicholson, 1928 (Pill Creek)
19½ x 24 in (49.5 x 61 cm) © Angela Verren Taunt.
All rights reserved, DACS 2018

*'In 1928 came the first paintings to show undoubted authority. In these he turned again to landscape, sometimes painting together with his friend Christopher Wood. There were not many pictures that year, but amongst them seemed to me to be his first unquestionable masterpieces. One of them is Pill Creek ... Perhaps the first thing to strike the spectator is the sense of movement, the eye is led into the picture at the lower left corner and swept happily along the lines of the stream, with the boat on the creek beyond as its goal. There may be pleasant excursions in the wood en route, but always the eye returns to the stream until the boat is reached; then the lines of the creek itself pointing back into the wood.'* [25]

**Joseph and Mary of Truro. circa 1860**
Private Collection
Michele Funno
*Italian, (active c.1837-1865) Naples.*

Alfred Wallis's paintings are unlike the work of the artists around him. From the start he was 'his own man' which is quite remarkable; but if one were to look for an influence, perhaps one could be found in the ship portrait paintings that were to be seen in so many St Ives Cottages at that time.

When visiting major ports, the vessel's master would likely have encountered a ship-portrait artist proffering examples of his work, seeking a commission to make a portrait of the ship. Such pierhead painters are known to have operated in Mediterranean ports, but Naples in particular became well known as a centre for ship-portrait painting. The background of these paintings often included topographical details, and in many Naples paintings Vesuvius was depicted smouldering in the distance. These paintings were brought back to their homes by the seamen to become lasting mementos of their voyage and their ship.

*Pictures of Vesuvius always in full eruption decorated the front rooms of many cottages in 19th century Newquay and St Ives. Many of these paintings of west country schooners in full sail in the Bay of Naples, still exist, pictures made by Italian artists for a few shillings and brought home to adorn Cornish firesides for generations.* [26]

**Three-masted Ship and Lighthouse**
Oil and pencil on card 4 x 7 in (10.2 x 17.8 cm) Private Collection

Undoubtedly Wallis's paintings were, as he put it 'out of my own memory', but some could have had a different source of inspiration. Ben Nicholson gave two illustrated books to Wallis, *In the Wake of the Wind Ships* by Frederick William Wallace, published by Hodder & Stoughton 1927 and *The Last of the Wind Ships* by Alan J Villiers, published by George Rutledge & Sons Ltd., 1934, which is illustrated with over 200 black and white photographs. It tells the story of a voyage from Australia to Falmouth made by the large sailing ship *Parma*. There are obvious similarities between this painting and the photographs, where the ship is seen from the starboard quarters. Wallis seems to have struggled to paint the ship at what was, for him, an unusual angle, which involved an element of perspective.

*Facing pages taken from* The Last of the Wind Ships.

# A Spirit of Freedom

For Ben and Winifred Nicholson, Wallis's work consolidated ideas that were running through their paintings at that time. In Cumberland, Ben Nicholson had already produced some simple, almost childlike landscapes early in 1928. 'One was wanting to get right back to the beginning, and then take a step at a time on a firm basis.' Later, Nicholson would be vocal about Wallis's influence on the development of his own visual language.

This group of artists was not alone in recognising the qualities of naïve or primitive art. The German Expressionists clearly displayed a love of the uninhibited and primitive, and Picasso learnt much from Iberian, African and Oceanic sculpture, as well as from the naïve painter Henri Rousseau. But Wallis's influence went beyond the purely visual. For his admirers, he came to represent an attitude, an idea that

*real creativity was direct and innate, that the imagination was fettered by training, that a painting was more importantly a thing in itself than a representation of something else, that strength of expression and vitality of working were more important than accuracy of description and technical skill, that the child, the primitive and the modern artist were somehow joined.* [27]

Most of the qualities that are valued in Wallis's work came naturally to him; his work was intuitive. His primary concern was to communicate the things that he knew about and had experienced, but in doing so he demonstrated his awareness of the fundamental concerns of the painter, finding ways to represent three dimensions on a flat surface. He used the shape, materiality and colour of the board itself as an integral part of his work, and his paintings are not just views but objects in their own right. In common with medieval art, primitive art and child art, Wallis's work has the ability to explore and communicate a deeper truth.

One of the people who remembered Wallis described how

*on fine days Wallis would put his paintings outside his cottage in Back Road West, St Ives, and explain to passers-by what they were, details of sails and what every part was used for - and the ropes. It was his way of being an old fisherman airing his knowledge, and this account serves to emphasise the entirely literal, factual approach which Wallis adopted in his work. He was never in the least interested in painting pretty pictures.* [28]

**Three-masted Schooner Near a Lighthouse**

Oil and watercolour on board 29½ x 20⅞ in (75 x 53 cm) Kettle's Yard, University of Cambridge

*'A great ship anchored in harbour, with that strange immobility and over-life-size feeling, common to ships standing in quiet water. It has a desolate assertiveness in which it is almost impossible to sense its cutting activity once it is on the high seas. Masts are perpendicular and sails are furled, looking like snow on all the crossbars. In picture after picture Wallis conveys the varied movement of a ship - the sea being all about it, lighthouses at an angle, land looming darkly overhead, salt and spray and the feather lightness of a ship, as compared with the vast weight of the sea in which it moves.'* H.S. Ede

**A Path Through a Wood**
Oil and pencil on an artist's paintbox 11¾ x 14½ in (29.9 x 36.8 cm)
Private Collection

**A Steamship and a Schooner Passing the Coast**
Oil and pencil on an artist's paintbox 11¾ x 14½ in (29.9 x 36.8 cm) Private Collection

*These two pictures were painted on the top and bottom of an artist's paintbox. There is a story of well-meaning people giving Wallis a box of oil paints, only for him to throw away the paints, preferring to use his familiar ship's enamel. However, the gift was not wasted: he painted on the box. These paintings were purchased from Wallis in 1937. The family story of the sale relates that the purchaser, who worked at the Leach Pottery, had reserved the paintings during the week but had returned to pay for them on Sunday. Wallis was furious and told him that money should not change hands on the Sabbath. The purchaser was obliged to go back for the paintings the following day.*

**Three-Master with sea birds**

Oil and pencil on blotter 10½ x 12 in (26.7 x 30.5 cm) Private Collection

*Painted on an old ink blotter.*

**Barque with man at the wheel on a stormy sea**
Oil on card 6¾ x 14⅝ in (17 x 37.2 cm)
Kettle's Yard, University of Cambridge

**Two Masted Schooner and A Lighthouse**
Pencil and oil on cardboard 20¼ x 24¾ in (51.4 x 62.9 cm)
Image courtesy of Sotheby's

For Wallis, an isolated character who was regarded as eccentric by the locals, meeting Wood and the Nicholsons obviously had a hugely encouraging effect. One could speculate that without this patronage Wallis could have remained unrecognised and his work lost. He often made three or four paintings a day, and must have produced several thousand pieces of work in the seventeen years that he was painting.

As Ben Nicholson said, Wallis's paintings were simple, direct and honest. Painting was the sole outlet for his feelings, and far from being 'pretty pictures', his paintings frequently express a sense of anxiety. It has been said that the portrayal of a ship symbolises the journey of the human soul from birth to death. Wallis paints ships climbing huge Atlantic swells, which as well as representing a vivid memory, aptly expresses the concept of 'facing adversity'.

**Three Figures On A Sailing Ship**
Image courtesy of Bonham's

*Full of life and energy, Alfred Wallis paintings lift our spirits, but they also evoke a variety of moods, at times dark and mysterious and sometimes, as in this painting, joyous; the sea is alive, and achieved with such simple means.*

Wallis has become recognised as one of the most original artists of the twentieth century. For generations of artists that were to follow, his work embodies the spirit of freedom that runs throughout the work of the St Ives modernists. It is all the more remarkable for the fact that this freedom of expression came from a man who was, as Mullins said, 'locked up darkly within himself ... whose daily life was exceptionally close to his moral and religious beliefs. He lived strictly within the narrow corridors of his life'.

Before joining the Royal Air Force in the Second World War, Peter Lanyon bought a painting from Wallis, who told him that he could have it on the condition that he read the Bible every day. When he asked about a detail in another painting he was told to mind his own business.

# Letters

A few months after their return to London, Ben and Winifred Nicholson were living in Dulwich when they began to receive parcels of paintings from Wallis. On the 19th November 1928, Wallis wrote to them:

*I am sendin on a Nother parcle.*

*He used to post us parcels of paintings done up in many sheets of old brown paper, criss-crossed and knotted with a thousand pieces of string, and it was always exciting opening these parcels to see what good ones might be inside.* (Ben Nicholson).

Ben Nicholson gave Wallis two books: *In the Wake of the Wind-ships* by Frederick William Wallace and *The Last of the Wind Ships* by Alan J. Villiers, and on 5th of December 1928 Wallis wrote: 'Sir, i Receved The Book all Rite'. Wallis's letters to Nicholson continue at intervals until at least 1934 (many have not survived).

The letters accompanying the paintings sent by Wallis to the Nicholsons and Jim Ede are written in the copperplate script that was taught in Wallis's schooldays, and they provide an insight into his attitude to his art. Despite the peculiar spelling and erratic use of capitals, his letters convey a profound awareness that he was recording a way of life gone for ever. For instance, in a letter to Ede he writes:

*what i do mosley is what use To Bee ... what we may never see again*

Furthermore, Wallis was aware that he was not the same as the other artists in St Ives whom he termed 'Real Artists'. In 1936 he wrote to Ede:

*i am self Taught so you Cannot me like Thouse That have Been Taught Both in school and paint i have had To learn myself i never go out To paint nor i never show Them.*

From alfred Wallis St ives
Feb 12 1934

sir i have sent on a Parcle us They are Tray i think They will do as They are what used to Be most all i do is what use to Be in ships and Boats what you phrape what you will never see aney any more i like sailin Craff.
Best for Looks

So i must tlos wishiny you good speed From your friend
alfred Wallis

**Letter to Ede**
Tate, London

April 1935

Dear sir i Receved
your letter with Thanks
and also The pantins Wich you
Did not want
what i do mosley is what
use To Bee out of my own
memery what we may never
see again as Thing are altered
all To gether Ther is nothin
what Ever do not look like
what it was sence i Can Rember
if i live Till The 8 of august
next i shall Be 78 years Old
i was Born in Devenport
Born on The day of The fall
of Sernveserpool Rushan
So i Cos from your war
       friend alfred wallis

November 4 1936

Mr Hede
i Receved Your letter
and The Returned parse
with Thanks Mr Ede
i never see any Thing
i send you now it is
what i have seen Before
i am self Taught so you
Cannot me like Thouse
That have Been Taught
Both in school and paint
i have had To learn my
self i never go out To paur
nor i never shaw Them
      from your friend
3 Back Roud alfred wallis
             St Ives

3 Back Road ur

Jun 10 1936

Dear sir i Receved your letter and Cheques and also the pictwrs you did not want op in your pleased i got a few Smaler

i do not know weather They will suit or not i do not shaw any nor offer any for Sale
The one with The Boats and harbour The Saynes shut is what used To Be all died out a litt of Defferan To what it wse To Be here it mest Be a gret Change for it To B as it was so i mest Clos wishin you well from your friend alfred wallis

ap 1 1936

Dear Sir i Receved your letter and Checqu all Right With Thanks glad you Receved The paintins The most you get is what use To Be all i do is hout of my mery
i do not go out any where To Draw and i Show any nor Offer any for sal Their is only 3 or 4 That have had ae i have don i got Som large ones But They will not go By Post The one with The Crab pots and fish is serpos To Be at The Bottom
i must Clos wishen you good spead opin your well from your True friend alfred wallis

**Boats with Lobster Pots**
Private Collection

**Fishes and Lobster Pots**
Oil on card 8⅝ x 18⅛ in (22 x 46 cm)
Kettle's Yard, University of Cambridge

*His years at sea in sailing ships and particularly fishing boats gave Wallis an awareness of what lies beneath the surface, as these paintings show. In his letter (opposite) he says: 'The one with The Crab pots and fish is serpos To Be at the Bottom'.*

A little insight into Wallis's personality is revealed in this correspondence. A December 1935 letter to Dorothy Elmhurst from Jim Ede, writing from the Tate, runs:

*Dear Dorothy, I wonder if you got the pictures by Wallace [sic] and whether you want to keep them. I'm sorry to bother you and to seem impatient, but I like at once to tell him what I am taking and to send him back the rest with the money. He gets all hot and bothered if he does not hear about by return!!*

A September 1936 letter from Wallis to Nicholson shows the former obviously somewhat impatient and anxious that he has not had a reply, revealing how much he needed reassurance and appreciation.

*sep 16*
*1936*
*Sir have you Receved*
*The Parcle of Paints i halways*
*like To know That people Receved*
*what i send Them and Weather*
*you like Them or not if you have*
*Receved Them pleas leave know*
*i put my adress inside So i should*
*like To know That you Receved Them*
*yours Truly alfred*
*wallis*
*no 3 Back Road w*
*St Ives Cornwall*

The Winifred Nicholson Archive

april 27
1937

Dear Mr Ede
Reeved your letter
and Chucks all Right
glad your pleased
i leave all To You You know with
how To mange Better Then i
i alway like to know do
That The parcel is Received
all Right The Bigone is
from St Ives Town To Lands
and longl ships 3 Mile off End
from The Lands End

Iuly 30
1938
Mr Ede
i have aBout 30 or 40
pantins They must
go By Train Somone
fetch Them if Their
was any Coming from
your place They Could
Call and Take Them
away i want Them
Cleard out i do not
know how soon i shall
have To moove The house
wants a great Repare
i think Their They are So
good if not Better i have
don They are Two mwany
for To send By Post

# Events

Encouraged by the interest in his work, painting became an all-absorbing passion for Wallis. His paintings were clearly drawn from his memories, but some current events found their way directly into his work.

**Six Ships**
Private Collection

*Photograph of the Grand Fleet.*
Photo: Private Collection

**The Grand Fleet**

This photograph shows part of the Grand Fleet, which anchored in Mount's Bay in late July 1910. St Michael's Mount is on the left. Before the First World War, ships of the Royal Navy serving in the Atlantic and the North Sea were painted dark grey, whilst those serving in other theatres were light grey. *Six Ships* could have been inspired by the sight of the Grand Fleet in Mount's Bay. If so, Wallis, painting many years later, has remembered this important detail.

*Gustav Hamel flying over St Michael's Mount.*
Photo: St Ives Archive

*Above: Gustav Hamel flying, and on the ground, West Cornwall 1913.*
Photos: St Ives Archive

### Airships and Aeroplanes

Before the First World War, the people of Cornwall saw very little aviation activity, but there was one notable flight. In 1913, Gustav Hamel flew his Blériot type plane over Mount's Bay, Land's End and St Ives.

**Sailing Ship Aeroplane and Airship**
Oil on card 6⅜ x 14¼ in (16.2 x 36.2 cm) Private Collection

Since the outbreak of the First World War, Britain was dependent on the import of food and raw materials. By 1917, Germany's policy of unrestricted warfare against shipping found in British waters resulted in many ships being sunk, with the loss of thousands of lives. The huge damage to shipping caused by German submarines at that time was unsustainable.

It was recognised that U-boats were easier to spot from the air than from the sea, and a number of anti-submarine Royal Naval air stations were established around the coast of Britain to counter the menace. It became apparent that Cornwall's position bordering the Atlantic, English Channel and the Western Approaches was of strategic importance and an airbase was built at Predannack, near Mullion on the western side of the Lizard peninsula. Mullion was commissioned in 1917 and a number of airships were stationed there. They carried bombs, guns and depth charges, working in conjunction with the Royal Navy. They escorted convoys from the Isles of Scilly to Plymouth and they did indeed sink some enemy submarines.

Later, in 1917, aeroplanes were also stationed at Mullion. Like the airships, they patrolled both the north and south coasts of Cornwall and also carried bombs and guns, and worked in cooperation with the Royal Navy - communicating by radio. That year, sea-planes and flying boats were also stationed at Newlyn and on the island of Tresco in the Scilly Isles, to assist the anti-submarine programme.

These aircraft must have been a remarkable sight for the people of Cornwall who witnessed them during the war, and Wallis included airships and aeroplanes in his paintings of ships and fishing boats.

*Photographs of aeroplanes at Predannack taken by William Paul Birkbeck, a pilot officer in the Royal Flying Corps.*

Photos: Collection Dr Tim Rogers

*Photographs of airships at Predannack taken by William Paul Birkbeck, a pilot officer in the Royal Flying Corps.*

Photos: Collection Dr Tim Rogers

*Bottom left: RAF Airship, Bonython c.1918.*

Iced Sponges

Private Collection

Boat with Plane and Airship

Private Collection

**The Wreck of Cicelia**

On 25th January 1935, not long before the painting *St Ives Bay* (p179) was purchased, the ketch *Cicelia* was unloading coal on Smeaton's Pier when, in a north-north-westerly gale, the vessel broke loose. After colliding with other boats, it was washed out of the harbour and wrecked on Pedn Olva Point. Incidentally, before becoming a collier *Cicelia* was the last Channel Island-owned vessel involved in the Newfoundland cod trade.

*Cicelia wrecked on Pedn Olva Point, St Ives. 25th January 1935.*

Photos: St Ives Archive

**St Ives Bay**

*This painting is another version of the St Ives Bay theme. Godrevy Light and the Stones Rocks are at the right of the painting; a steamer passes on its way down the coast, and off the harbour two fishing boats are seen at anchor, their mizzen sails set to keep them to wind. At the bottom left of the picture, a sailing ship appears almost upside down.*

*Working on his paintings from different sides, Wallis often showed vessels at unusual angles, but we sense that this ship is in trouble. Of course, Wallis and the St Ives community would have been aware of the fate of the Bideford ketch* Cicelia, *which was the last sailing ship to be wrecked in St Ives Bay.*

**St Ives Bay**
Private Collection

## The Gale at St. Ives

### KETCH BREAKS ADRIFT IN HARBOUR

### WRECKED AT PEDNOLVER POINT

A fierce gale swept the country during the week-end and St. Ives came in for a full share of its force, the harbour especially being the scene of most of the havoc.

The Bideford ketch Cecilia, which arrived at St. Ives just over a fortnight ago, after parting her moorings, caused considerable damage to the pilots' small boat Julia; carried away with her jib-boom the wing of the bridge of the steamer Lady Thomas, which was alongside the pier; sank two or three punts, and caused a lamp standard on the quay to be broken.

The crew of the Cecilia, a vessel of 53 tons net register, on Saturday morning were strengthening the moorings, when the ropes and chains parted, and the vessel, after its erratic course, drifted on to the rocks at Pednolver, where she became a total wreck. Many people watched the helpless craft as she grounded within a few feet of the bedroom windows of some houses in the vicinity of the harbour.

*The St Ives Times, 31st January 1935.*

*Right:* Cicelia *wrecked on Pedn Olva Point, St Ives. 25th January 1935.*

Photos: St Ives Archive

### The Wreck of SS Alba

On 31st January 1938, the Panamanian freighter *Alba* went aground on Porthmeor Beach in a storm. The ship had been carrying a cargo of coal from South Wales to Italy. The St Ives lifeboat *Caroline Parsons* had successfully taken off twenty-three of the crew, but capsized and was washed onto the rocks near the wreck. Using torches and lamps rescuers managed to save all the members of the lifeboat crew but five of *Alba*'s crew died. Wallis undoubtedly witnessed this event, and made a number of paintings of the incident, showing the lifeboat aground on the rocks and the waves breaking over the wrecked ship. Remains of SS *Alba*'s boilers can still be seen on the Island side of Porthmeor beach at low spring tide.

*SS* Alba *and the wrecked lifeboat* Caroline Parsons *on the rocks on Porthmeor Beach.*
Photo: St Ives Archive
*It is thought that the captain of the* Alba *misread the lights of St Ives in storm conditions, in the belief that the ship was heading into the sheltered waters of the bay; instead they were wrecked on Three Brothers Rock, Porthmeor Beach.*

**The wreck of the Alba**

Oil on card 7¾ x 10 in (19.7 x 25.4 cm) Courtesy Crane Kalman Gallery

*The burial of the five crewmen of the Alba, Barnoon Cemetery, St Ives 1938.*

Photos: St Ives Archive

**The Wreck of the Alba**

Oil on board 14¾ x 26⅞ in (37.5 x 68.3 cm) Tate, London

*Reading from left to right, a steamship passes* Alba *wrecked on Porthmeor Beach and the wrecked lifeboat* Caroline Parsons. *The Island St Ives with the medieval St Nicholas Chapel at the top. Across St Ives Bay is Godrevy Lighthouse and Hayle Estuary, bottom right.*

**The Wreck of the Alba**
Oil on card 10¾ x 13¼ in (27.3 x 33.8 cm)
Kettle's Yard, University of Cambridge

*SS Alba wrecked on Porthmeor Beach, St Ives, 1938.*
Photo: St Ives Archive

**the wreck of the Alba**
Oil on card 10½ x 13¼ in (26.5 x 33.5 cm)
Kettle's Yard, University of Cambridge

*Lifeboat* John and Sarah Eliza Stych *wrecked near Godrevy.*
Photo: St Ives Archive

### The Wreck of the lifeboat John and Sarah Eliza Stych

Following the loss of the St Ives lifeboat *Caroline Parsons* in the SS *Alba* incident, the second lifeboat from Padstow, *John and Sarah Eliza Stych*, was loaned to St Ives. On the night of 23rd January 1939, the lifeboat was called out to attend a ship in trouble to the south west of the town. The lifeboat capsized three times in the storm-force conditions and was eventually washed onto the rocks on the other side of St Ives Bay, at Gwithian near Godrevy. Only one of the eight crew members survived. The loss was deeply mourned in St Ives.

> *Wallis was so upset by this event that he saved three weeks of his pension - his only means of livelihood at the time - and gave it to the lifeboat fund.* [29]

All that was found in the following days were some bits of wreckage of *SS Wilston* at Wicca Pool, some miles west of St Ives, near Zennor. The ship disappeared; there were no survivors.

**Godrevy, Lifeboat and Boats on the Rocks**

Oil on cardboard 7½ x 11¾ in (19 x 30 cm) Private Collection

*In this painting, Wallis surely tells us the story of that fateful night. On the left of the painting the ship SS* Wilston *lies wrecked against the cliffs. On the right is Godrevy Lighthouse and below that is the ill-fated lifeboat* John and Sarah Eliza Stych *being carried towards the coast by the storm.*
*At the bottom right of the painting, SS* Alba, *wrecked the previous year; nearby on the rocks, the wrecked lifeboat* Caroline Parsons.

### Ship Against the Rocks

Market House Gallery, Marazion

*Another painting featuring a wrecked ship. One has the feeling of looking down from a cliff on to a vessel that has clearly been washed on to the rocks.*

There is great power in the tidal movement of the seas, a fact of which seafarers and those who sail or fish for a living are always conscious. *Steamer in a Rough Sea*, opposite, is another painting that features Land's End and the Longships. The tides off the coast of Penwith towards Land's End are known to be particularly strong. The flags and buffs that mark crab pots and nets are drawn under the surface by the force of the tide. In these places, fishermen are only able to haul their gear in the period around slack tide at either high or low water.

As a seaman, Alfred Wallis must have been well aware of the strength of the tide, and it is apparent here. The steamship pushes against the force of the outgoing tide as it makes its way past the rocks of the Longships and heads up the coast of Penwith.

**Steamer in a Rough Sea**

Private Collection

*Painted in just three colours and utilising the background colour of the board, this painting is alive with a remarkable energy. This part of the coast features in several of Wallis's paintings; he clearly knew the waters of this area well.*

*SS* Bluejacket *wrecked on the Longships, 1898.*
Photo: Gibson & Sons, Courtesy of the Artist's Estate

### The Wreck of SS Bluejacket

The steamship *Bluejacket* ran onto the rocks close to the Longships Lighthouse on the night of 9th November 1898 in hazy conditions and a stiff easterly wind. *SS Bluejacket* had been heading to her home port of Cardiff from Plymouth, where she had delivered a cargo of railway sleepers. The Sennen Cove lifeboat rescued the crew, but attempts to save the steamer itself were unsuccessful. Note the large sailing vessel in the distance.

In 1898, Wallis was working in the Marine Stores. The wrecked ship remained on the rocks for over a year, so it is possible that Wallis could have seen it there, or perhaps a photograph of the event inspired his painting.

**Against Longships Fog** (inscribed with title)

Oil on card 11⅜ x 17⅛ in (29.5 x 43.5 cm) Pier Arts Centre, Orkney

*This painting features the area of Land's End and the Longships. The Longships Lighthouse and rocks are seen from the seaward side. A ship is wrecked on the rocks; behind, a steamship and a sailing vessel pass the coast of Land's End and Gwennap Head. The painting must relate to the Bluejacket incident as it is such an unlikely thing to have happened - after all, lighthouses are built to prevent this sort of occurrence.*

**Visiting Boats, East Coast Boats and Newlyn Riots**

Wallis's seagoing days were behind him and he was working in the Marine Stores in St Ives by 1896 when a series of dramatic events took place in Newlyn. At that time, Newlyn was home to one of the largest fishing fleets in the country and was a regular landing place for many vessels from other ports that fished in Cornish waters, in particular the fleets from Lowestoft, Suffolk and Great Yarmouth, Norfolk.

Like the fishermen of St Ives, many of the Newlyn fishermen held strong religious beliefs; as members of Methodist and Protestant religious groups they would not fish on the Sabbath. But unlike the Cornish, the crews from elsewhere in Britain often had no reservations about fishing on Sundays, and their catch fetched a better price on the Monday market. This put the local fishermen at a disadvantage in their home waters, and they felt aggrieved.

**Lowestoft Fishing Vessel**
Oil on card 4½ x 7 in (11.4 x 17.8 cm) Private Collection

Unrest had been apparent for a period, then things came to a head and riots broke out on Monday, 18th May 1896. A group of forty Newlyn fishermen, supported by a thousand local people, boarded the visiting boats and threw the Sunday-caught fish into the harbour.

Running battles between the two groups ensued, and about a hundred police arrived at the scene. Violent clashes between the police and the fishermen took place on the following day and several hundred soldiers were sent to the area by rail. The riots were eventually quelled when a Royal Naval gunship came to Newlyn harbour, threatening to destroy Cornish fishing boats before compromise fishing agreements between the local and visiting fishermen were reached.

**A Schooner Under Full Sail**

Oil and pencil on card 6 x 13¾ in (15.2 x 34.9 cm) Image courtesy of Sotheby's

*The title of this painting is misleading. As the letters on the sail indicate, it depicts a fishing vessel from Great Yarmouth. In the latter part of the nineteenth century, fishing fleets from that port and Lowestoft were drawn to the rich fishing around Cornwall.*

**Two Sailing Boats Entering the Harbour**
Oil on cardboard 8 x 15¾ in (20.3 x 40 cm) Image courtesy of Christie's

**Ships Entering Harbour**
Private Collection
*Crayon on paper. In this drawing Wallis remembers the LT registered fishing boats that came from Lowestoft to fish Cornish waters.*

### Brixham Sailing Trawlers

Brixham is a port on the south coast of Devon, where a method of fishing the seabed by towing a large net attached to a beam was developed. It was known as beam trawling. Between 1880 and 1920, a great many sailing beam trawlers came from Brixham and Dartmouth and fished around the coast of Britain. Some of these vessels were based in Newlyn, and would have been known to Wallis. They were either ketch or sloop rigged and Wallis remembers both rigs in his paintings.

*Brixham trawlers waiting for a breeze in 1868.*
Photo: Royal Cornwall Museum

**Two Sailing Ships & Lighthouse**

Oil, pencil and wash on paper 11 x 15 in (27.9 x 38.1 cm)
Image courtesy of Sotheby's

*In this painting and photograph, the beam trawls can be seen on the deck overhanging the sterns of the boats.*

*Brixham trawlers at sea. 19th century.*
Photo: Royal Cornwall Museum

Two Boats

Jerwood Collection

### French Fishing Boats

French crabbers from Brittany first came from Cameret in 1902 to fish the Scillies and the north coast of Cornwall and became a feature of the summer scene in Newlyn, St Ives and Newquay. They fished with crab pots for crayfish, lobster and crab, and their vessels had wet wells to keep the shellfish alive until they returned to Brittany. This practice continued until the mid 1960s.

The early French crabbers were sailing vessels and were gaff rigged, but in these paintings Wallis recalls lug-sailed vessels. Christopher Wood also painted French fishing boats in Brittany on his visits there in 1929 and 1930.

*French fishing boats in Newlyn Harbour.*

**French Fishin Boat** (inscribed with title)
Oil on card 6⅞ x 11½ in (17.5 x 29 cm) Image courtesy of Lawrences

**French Lugsail Fishin Boat** (inscribed with title)
Oil on card 6⅞ x 15¾ in (17.5 x 40 cm)
Kettle's Yard, University of Cambridge

*Caprice of Camaret (J. Saint Cyr)*

# Wallis's Vision

**Maps of the Sea**

Alfred Wallis did not use an easel; he painted at a table in his living room. No doubt, he sat at the table to make the smaller paintings, but for larger works he must have been standing and looking at his painting from above. In his imagination, he hovered over the land and sea, as, years later, Peter Lanyon would later experience the Atlantic coast and Cornish landscape from his glider.

Wallis's paintings of St Ives Bay, Mounts Bay and Falmouth Bay are map-like - or more particularly - chart-like. They are 'maps of the sea' and of course Wallis must have been familiar with nautical charts from his seagoing days.

*Since the 1870s schooner and ketch masters seem always to have used charts, both in deep water and in the home trade.* [30]

One can look down at St Ives from various high vantage points; the harbours of Newlyn and Penzance can also be seen from elevated positions, yet somehow one senses that these paintings do not arise solely from direct observation but come from Wallis's ability to visualise the geography of the sea and coast he knew so well and that had remained in his memory.

Working in this way, looking down on his creations, we can see that he was able to turn the painting or move around it to work from different sides. As an untrained artist, Wallis was not only free from the constraints of conventional perspective, he was unrestricted by the convention of creating a painting from a fixed viewpoint.

Wallis was completely unaware of developments in modern painting or abstraction, yet working alone at his table in the front room of his cottage in Back Road West he was making paintings from multiple viewpoints - an idea central to the Cubist works of Picasso and Braque.

In his paintings, he looks down on St Ives Bay; land and sea are tipped up in what has been described as a flattening of the picture plane, yet the images are not 'flat'. Wallis has his own sense of space and depth; the interplay between flatness and depth and between surface and illusion is fascinating.

With their elevated viewpoints, this tipping up and flattening brings an awareness of the pictorial design and emphasises the abstract elements in the Wallis's work. Here we can see a direct link to the abstraction of the St Ives Modernist Movement that was to follow.

*Smeaton's Pier, designed by civil engineer John Smeaton, is located on the northern side of St Ives harbour and was constructed between 1767 and 1770. The pier was originally 360 feet long with the elegant Smeaton's lighthouse sitting at the end. However, in the 1890s the pier was extended to almost double its length and a new lighthouse added. The original lighthouse is now known as The Middle Lighthouse.*

**St Ives Harbour, Hayle Bay and Godrevy and Fishing Boats 1932-4**

Oil on card 25¼ x 18 in (64.1 x 45.7 cm) Private Collection

*The tide is out and the rocks of the Stones Reef, marked by Godrevy Lighthouse, are visible (at high tide they are covered by the sea). The boats lie at their moorings on the sand in the harbour. Schooners lie next to Smeaton's Pier with the three arches at the top. The 'middle lighthouse' and the lighthouse are shown. Smaller pilchard drivers are moored ahead of the larger mackerel drivers and a variety of pleasure boats are seen next to the West Pier. At the bottom left of the painting is the Stennack River, and on the right is Hayle Estuary, the channel marked by the Bar Buoy. The estuary can be treacherous and many ships have come to grief there, as Wallis shows.*

**St Ives Bay Paintings**

Wallis returned to the theme of St Ives Bay many times in paintings that are among the most poetic of all his work. Most of the St Ives Bay pieces have a similar format. On the right is Godrevy Island with its lighthouse. This lighthouse provides a warning of the Stones, a dangerous reef which extends a mile and a half seaward from the island. The lighthouse is also a beacon for vessels bound for St Ives and the port of Hayle.

The left-hand side of each picture is occupied by the harbour of St Ives, with Smeaton's Pier and its lighthouse at the end. In most of the paintings, Wallis has shown the building half way down the quay, originally the lighthouse on the end of the pier, now known as the 'middle lighthouse'.

The objects protruding from the shore at the bottom of the paintings are seine nets, and the seine-netting boats are pulled up on the strand.

An intensely religious man, Wallis's faith gave meaning and structure to his life. He drew comfort and security from his beliefs, and lived a simple and frugal existence in his later years, painting every day. Through his vision, we sense the presence of God from the Christian Bible he would read each day, and all day on Sunday. These paintings, in particular, convey an almost spiritual message. Perhaps Wallis is saying that 'God looked down on St Ives Bay and saw that all was well'.

In the bottom right-hand corner is Hayle Estuary, the entrance to the port of Hayle, and Lelant Saltings, used as a safe harbour by the fishing fleet in winter and poor weather. Although vessels are safe once inside the harbour, the mouth of the estuary is noted for its dangerous sand bar. Many boats have come to grief going over the bar, and it is essential to know where the channel through to the harbour is, and it is marked by the Bar Buoy. The buoy would be unimportant to someone not connected with the sea, but for the seaman it is an essential feature, and it appears in most of Wallis's paintings of St Ives Bay.

Merchant ships carrying cargoes to and from the port of Hayle were a common sight in those days. In the eighteenth and nineteenth centuries, Hayle was a thriving port and an industrial town, the main firms being the Cornish Copper Company and Harvey & Co. Ltd. The latter was a considerable business consisting of a foundry, an iron works and a shipbuilder, manufacturing beam engines and a variety of machinery for the Cornish tin mine industry. The engines it was making were at the forefront of technology in the early days of the Industrial Revolution, and were exported all over the world. Many vessels visited Hayle, particularly those bringing coal and pig iron from Wales. The coal was used to fuel the furnaces and the pumping engines of the mines. Timber, limestone and agricultural produce, particularly grain, were also shipped to Hayle.

**St Ives Bay and Godrevy**

Oil and pencil on card 10¾ x 17¾ in (27.3 x 45 cm) Private Collection

*In the latter part of the nineteenth century, St Ives Bay was a busy place. In addition to its large fishing fleet, merchant sail and steamships would call at St Ives and Hayle, arriving with such cargoes as coal, salt and timber, and departing with tin, copper ore and salt pilchards.*

*In many of the paintings of St Ives Bay, Wallis shows the wooden jetty known as the New Pier, built in the 1860s. It lasted only twenty years, having been irreparably damaged in storms.*

Photos: St Ives Archive

**St Ives Harbour and Godrevy** - also called **Three Ships and Lighthouse**

Oil and pencil on card 12⅝ x 18¼ in (32 x 46.5 cm) Pier Arts Centre, Orkney

*Smeaton's Pier before the extension was built in the 1890s.*
Photo: St Ives Archive

**St Ives Bay**
Crayon on paper. Private Collection
*One of the many sketchbook drawings Wallis made during the last fourteen months of his life in Madron Public Assistance Institute.*

**Steamers at Harbour Entrance**
Oil and pencil 9¼ x 13 in (23.5 x 33 cm) Image courtesy of Bonham's

### St Ives Harbour

Oil on mahogany board 19 x 34¼ in (48.3 x 87 cm)
Crane Kalman Gallery, London
*In 1936 Adrian Stokes took this piece of wood
(19" x 36") to Wallis for him to paint on.*

**The Seine Fishery**

The history of the Cornish fishing industry has been shaped by the abundance of one particular fish, the pilchard. Pilchards were caught in drift nets from luggers, or by seine nets using two large rowing boats, a method unique to Devon and Cornwall. The pilchard is a member of the herring family, and in late summer and autumn large shoals swept along the coast, where they could be surrounded by a seine net.

There is nothing to suggest that Alfred Wallis was actively involved in the seine fishing industry of St Ives. However, he was certainly aware of this unique fishery and its importance to the town. Wallis's paintings of St Ives Bay feature the seine nets and boats at Porthminster Beach, and for this reason it is worth understanding what the fishery involved.

The pilchard seining season began each year in late July or early August, when the seine boats were launched from Porthminster beach, where they had been laid up since the previous season. Overlooking St Ives Bay stands the huers' hut, from which a constant lookout was kept by 'huers' for the pilchard shoals during the season; their presence marked by characteristic red-brown patches of their oil on the surface of the water. When a shoal was spotted, the call of 'Hevva!' (they're here) would sound throughout the town, summoning the seine fishermen. The huers guided the seine boats, which were manned by six oarsmen and a cox, to the shoal by signalling with 'bushes' made from pieces of gorse covered with canvas. When the boats were close to the shoal, the huer would shout through his trumpet to shoot the seine net around the shoal. This was a scene of great excitement because many tons of fish could be encircled in as little as an hour or so. This was obviously a tricky and sensitive operation, and trains coming to St Ives were forbidden to sound their whistle during the season.

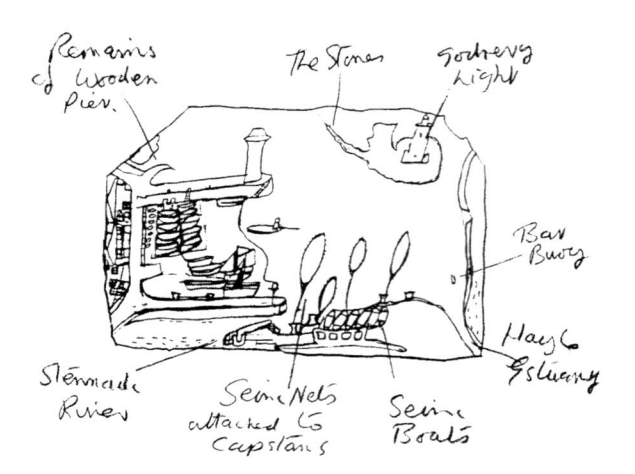

**This is Sain Fishery That Used To Be**

Oil and pencil on card 15 x 22½ in (40.6 x 57.1 cm) Private Collection

Some pilchards were sold fresh, but most of the fish were taken to curing cellars to be salted before being packed into barrels known as 'hogsheads'. Each hogshead contained four and a half hundredweight, about 3,000 fish. Once packed, they were exported to Spain, France and Italy.

In 1869, St Ives alone had 260 seine nets. In the year 1871, 43,000 hogsheads of cured pilchards were exported from the town. This was an extraordinary amount of fish, and even though this was an exceptional year, it gives some idea of the capacity of the industry at the time. Virtually the entire community was in some way involved, and it was certainly a time when St Ives smelled of fish - rather than fish and chips. The Reverend Francis Kilvert, on a visit to Cornwall, noted in his diary: 'The vicar of St Ives says the stench there is so terrific as to stop the church clock.'

The building of the railway line to Penzance and the branch line to St Ives in 1877 had opened new markets, and fishing activity intensified, but towards the end of the century catches declined. By the early years of the twentieth century, the pilchards had practically disappeared. 'From the end of the 19th century seining in St Ives was in sharp decline. The last successful seine was in 1908, and 1922 was the last year in which watch was kept for the shoals by the huers at Porthminster Point.' [31]

Wallis's awareness of the decline in the pilchard fishing industry gives poignancy to the title of his painting *This is the Sain Fishery That Use To Be*, and to his statement: 'What i do mosly is what use To Bee out of my own memery what we may never see again as Thing are altered all To gether Ther is nothin what Ever do not look like what it was since i Can Rember.' [32]

**St Ives with Godrevy Lighthouse**
Oil on card 6¾ x 37½ in (17.1 x 95.2 cm) Private Collection

**Harbour with Two Lighthouses and Motor Vessel**

Oil on card 20 x 25¼ in (51 x 64 cm) Kettle's Yard, University of Cambridge

*Above:* Huer with telescope.

*Top right:* The huer at work - a scene of great excitement.

*Bottom right:* A seine fishing boat shoots its nets around a shoal of pilchards.

Photos: St Ives Archive

*Scenes from the seine fishery when huge amounts of pilchards were encircled. c1880.*

Photos: St Ives Archive

*The process of taking the pilchards from the nets is called tucking.*
Photo: St Ives Archive

*Pilchards being pressed into barrels known as hogsheads.*
Photos: St Ives Archive

*A train arrives at St Ives station. The seine boats are laid up on Porthminster Beach awaiting the call of 'Heva'. During the seine season the train was not allowed to sound its whistle for fear of frightening off the shoals of pilchards.*
Photo: St Ives Archive

*Seine boats lined up by the railway line, Porthminster.*
Photo: St Ives Archive

# The Last Years

Photo: Private Collection

**Madron**

In 1937, Alfred Wallis was knocked down by what he believed to be the mayor's car in the Digey - the street that runs from Back Road West and Porthmeor Beach to the town. In a letter to Jim Ede, Wallis wrote: 'I can't stand this knocking about' and referred to his accident as being 'Knocked Down by a Motor Car in The Street' or having been 'Thron under Motor Car'. Berlin notes that Wallis 'was very badly shaken up and was never quite the same afterwards. His age at that time was eighty-two.

A small man, Wallis was often teased by children. On one occasion, after visiting Penzance he got off the train at Marazion and walked home, a distance of about ten miles, having been upset by boys on the train. He was eighty-four. There are other reports of boys throwing stones at him.

As Wallis grew older, he became increasingly deaf and isolated. He heard voices from a female figure he named 'Dooty Mighty', whom he associated with his deceased wife, and who 'told him what to do'. Suspicious and paranoid, he saw the wireless and chimney as conduits for the Devil, yet in June 1941 he was delighted to be visited by Peter Lanyon, Barbara Hepworth and Ben Nicholson during a 'studio open day'.

Shortly after, a doctor attending him for bronchitis reported his condition to the authorities and, aged almost eighty-six, he went into Madron Public Assistance Institute.

*'Wallis made no resistance "I don't care where I go to be looked after" he said, and when the time came he was dressed up and waiting to be taken away. He took only his watch, his magnifying glass and his scissors.'* [33]

Berlin said that Wallis spent the first month in bed, but when he got up he asked for painting materials. His condition improved, and it is possible that he benefitted from the communal life at the institute. He was able to draw and paint again and was visited by his artist friends, who brought him sketchbooks, pencils and paint.

To begin with, other residents treated his paintings with ridicule, but after a visit by Ben Nicholson who took along a catalogue, *Cahiers d'Art*, featuring Wallis and an appreciation of his work by Herbert Read as evidence to show he was a famous artist, their attitude changed.

Alethea Garstin visited Wallis in Madron in 1941,

*'and in one of the long rooms where the inmates lived, there was this old prophet - they had let his hair grow long ... one of them said to me in a serious tone of voice, "this gentleman is an artist"!'* [34]

*Madron Workhouse.*
Photo: St Ives Archive

*Madron Workhouse was built on the hills above Penzance in 1838 as a place where the poor could live and work. It served the villages and towns of west Cornwall and could accommodate 400. After 1930, the workhouse became Madron Public Assistance Institute and by the time Wallis went there the conditions had improved since its workhouse days, and it was more of a home for the elderly poor.*

### Sketchbooks

Wallis's artist friends brought him sketchbooks, paint and drawing materials when they visited him in Madron Public Assistance Institute. During the last fourteen months of his life in Madron, Alfred Wallis filled the sketchbooks with paintings and drawings on both sides of the page.

Sven Berlin later categorised some of the sketchbooks as the *Castle book*, the *Lion book* and the *Grey book*. Ben Nicholson gave him a scrapbook, known as the *Derwent* scrapbook, which was exhibited in the 1968 Penwith and Tate exhibitions. Later, Wills Lane Gallery sold individual pages from the scrap-book separately. The drawing (below), depicts a barque passing a coast and lighthouse (Penwith and the Longships) For many years it belonged to the St Ives sculptor Denis Mitchell.

**Sailing ship and lighthouse** 1942

11 x 16 in (28 x 40 cm) Private Collection

*A page from the Derwent scrapbook, which was given to Alfred Wallis by Ben Nicholson when Wallis was in the Madron Public Assistance Institute. Wallis filled it with paintings and drawings. The scrapbook was included in the 1968 Arts Council exhibition (lent by Mrs Adrian Stokes). It was subsequently owned by Sven Berlin and then by Wills Lane Gallery where it was broken up and pages sold individually. This drawing was owned by Denis Mitchell for many years.*

*Paintings and drawings from the Grey Book* 9¼ x 12 in (23.5 x 30 cm)

*Paintings and drawings from the Grey Book* 9¼ x 12 in (23.5 x 30 cm)

*Paintings and drawings from the Grey Book* 9¼ x 12 in (23.5 x 30 cm)

221

*Paintings and drawings from the Grey Book* 9¼ x 12 in (23.5 x 30 cm)

*Drawings from the Lion Book* 8½ x 11½ in (21.5 x 29 cm)

*Drawings from the Lion Book* 8½ x 11½ in (21.5 x 29 cm)

*Drawings from the Lion Book* 8½ x 11½ in (21.5 x 29 cm)

*Drawing from the Lion Book* 8½ x 11½ in (21.5 x 29 cm)

*In this drawing Wallis recalls the wreck of the sailing ship John Gray. Here he also describes Penzance Harbour; the South Quay with its lighthouse, the inner harbour and, at a the bottom of the drawing, the Ross Bridge. The rocks he depicts on the right of the south quay are surely Battery Rocks, now the site of the Art Deco Jubilee Swimming pool.*

Before he was admitted to Madron Public Assistance Institute Alfred Wallis's health was clearly in decline, but after a month there his condition improved, and in the last year of his life he produced a series of works in the sketchbooks supplied by his artist friends. These direct and spontaneous drawings are full of the life and energy we associate with Wallis's work.

The Grey, Lion and Castle Books were part of a private collection. The Grey Sketchbook was exhibited along with the Derwent Scrapbook in the 1968 Arts Council exhibition curated by Sir Alan Bowness. Now in the public realm, they were the catalyst for the 1920-21 Wallis exhibition at Kettle's Yard.

Alfred Wallis once again demonstrates his extraordinary visual memory, and one can see how the images in the sketchbooks relate to his earlier paintings; the Royal Albert Bridge, lightships, luggers and a variety of sailing ships, steamships with smoke flying, gulls, and of course St Ives, Mount's Bay and the harbours of Penzance and Newlyn. In two drawings (one in the Lion Book and another in the Castle Book) in coloured-pencil drawings he recalls one of his favourite subjects, Mount's Bay.

In the drawing above we see the familiar features of the Lizard Light, Mullion, Porthleven, the Mount, and on the left, one of several low-lying rocks, which lie just off shore and are only visible at low tide.

*Drawing from the Castle Book* 8½ x 11 in (21.5 x 28 cm)

He has featured these rocks in other paintings, but here is something we have not seen before. A sailing ship on the rocks!

Over the years many ships have come to grief on this piece of coast having been driven ashore in gales, but the drawing in the Castle Book indicates that Wallis was describing a specific event, as above the ship on the rocks he has inscribed: *Wreck John Gray*.

Newspaper reports state that on 7th January 1867 a Glasgow registered barque John Gray was sailing from Demerara to London carrying a cargo of rum, molasses and sugar when it was driven into Mount's Bay by a tremendous gale and snowstorm and was wrecked. The drama went on for several hours and the rescue was witnessed by hundreds of local people. Thirteen crew were saved by the Penzance lifeboat Richard Lewis, but the ship's captain and mate lost their lives in the incident.

Alfred Wallis spent his childhood in Devonport, but in 1866 his mother Jane died of tuberculosis. Some time later his father returned to Penzance with his two sons. In January 1867, at the time of the John Gray incident, Alfred Wallis was eleven years old. Nearing the end of his life in Madron Institute, Wallis draws on a vivid boyhood memory to describe a real event.

*Wreck of John Gray, 7th January 1867*
Penzance lifeboat Richard Lewis. Engraving; London Evening News 1867. Photo archive; Morrab Library, Penzance.

*Drawing from the Castle Book*
8½ x 11 in (21.5 x 28 cm)

On 25 August 1942, fourteen months after being admitted to Madron and nineteen years after the death of Susan, Alfred Wallis died. He was eighty-six.

After Wallis's death, Stokes and Nicholson were given permission to go to his house to retrieve any paintings that Wallis had left there before the Relieving Officer burnt all his possessions. Together with Margaret Mellis, they collected nearly a hundred paintings and also managed to collect fleas. Margaret Mellis later wrote that on the way back to Carbis Bay

> *Ben got out and washed up to his neck in the sea with his natty blue shorts, white shoes and cap.*
> *He stayed in the sea until the fleas were dead.* **35**

Among the mourners at his funeral on 3 September were Ben Nicholson, Barbara Hepworth, Adrian Stokes, Margaret Mellis, Bernard Leach, Naum and Miriam Gabo. Flowers from Mr and Mrs Gabo were accompanied by a note: 'In homage to the artist on whom Nature has bestowed the rarest of gifts, not to know that he is one.'

If not for Adrian Stokes, Wallis would have had a pauper's burial. Stokes paid for the plot in Barnoon Cemetery and arranged for the Salvation Army to conduct the service. The position of the grave could not have been more fitting, overlooking Porthmeor Beach and with a commanding view of the Atlantic Ocean. Looking out to sea, to the left of the beach, is Clodgy Point where Wallis liked to walk, and on the right, the Island with St Nicholas Chapel and the town of St Ives and beyond Godrevy.

Bernard Leach made the ceramic tiles that decorate his grave. The inscription reads
ALFRED WALLIS ARTIST & MARINER
1855 aug 18 - aug 29 1942
INTO THY HANDS O LORD

# Appendix I
## Our view of Wallis

Those who are familiar with Wallis's work will be aware that he was often described as a semiliterate, paranoid, flea-ridden, ex-rag and bone man. Undeniably, he was unable to look after himself towards the end of his life, when he was infested with fleas and suffered from acute paranoid delusions.

As a religious man, God and the Devil were real to Wallis, and during his last days in Back Road West he seems to have been tormented by the demons of his imagination. However, as Dr Slack commented, Wallis suffered from senile decay. Such afflictions can make their claim on any of us, but artists' biographers do not generally dwell on their subject's senility. Yet in the case of Wallis, the focus on his condition in his declining years leaves the impression that he was in this state throughout his life.

### Never at sea

One particular matter raised by one of his distant relatives cast doubt on both Wallis's sanity and his honesty: the question of whether Wallis actually went to sea. Albert Ward Rowe, whose grandfather was Wallis's stepson, wrote of his childhood memories of Wallis in his book *The Boy and the Painter*. Rowe's story was broadcast on the BBC Home Service on 2nd August 1957 and later appeared in several magazines, including *Studio International*. It was also printed in the *St Ives Times & Echo* on 27th December 1957, thus colouring the local view of Wallis. Rowe recounts:

> *Now Grandfather had told me that Alfred had never been to sea in his life, but that because he wasn't exactly right in the head, he always talked as if he had.*

David Sylvester's article, *The old man and the sea-piece*, which appeared in the colour supplement of the *Sunday Times*, 31 January 1965, gave undue credibility to Albert Rowe's statement. Sylvester clearly valued Wallis's work, and he acknowledged the influence that it had on contemporary painting in this country. He recognised the direct effect it had on the work of Nicholson and Wood and that it 'deeply influenced' William Scott, Roger Hilton and Peter Lanyon. Nevertheless, he perpetuated the myth of the mad artist:

> *clearly Wallis was pretty mad, and not only in his old age when he gradually became stone deaf ... but it is likely that he never went to sea. In one of his broadcast talks of his Cornish childhood, A W Rowe, who was Wallis's great nephew, said that his grandfather had told him that Alfred had never been to sea but that, because he wasn't right in the head he always talked as if he had. It is true that Wallis was far from right in the head, but it must be allowed that Rowe's grandfather had been on nonspeaking terms with Wallis for many years and may possibly have been wanting to discredit him in the eyes of a small boy who rather liked him.*

**Never at sea**

Sir,—David Sylvester was kind enough to quote me at some length in his article on Alfred Wallis in last week's Magazine. I most strongly object, though, to his implying that my grandfather may possibly have been wanting to discredit Alfred in my eyes and so lied by telling me that Alfred had never been to sea in his life. Like many other Cornishmen of his generation, my grandfather lived by his Bible. He would not have lied about anything. During the years when artists and collectors were acquiring Alfred's pictures, my grandfather sent him his daily hot dinner, a substantial meal exactly the same as we ourselves had and which kept him from starving.

May I also correct Mr Sylvester on one other point: Alfred had no beard, but a fine, white, Crippen-like moustache.

A W Rowe
Hull

David Sylvester writes: I am sorry to have vexed Mr Rowe, to whom my article was greatly indebted. I thought I should allow for the faint possibility that Wallis's sea-going reminiscences were not completely delusional (he too was a devout Bible-reader) since a number of intelligent people who knew him are persuaded there was some truth in them.

Albert Rowe took issue with Sylvester's comments regarding his grandfather's motives and wrote to *The Times*. (Illustrated, left)

### Bill Wallis

In 2006, I was introduced to the grandson of Alfred Wallis's brother Charles, 87- year-old Bill Wallis. We talked about his memories of his great uncle Alfred from the late 1930s. It was the period before Bill joined the Royal Air Force during the Second World War and before Wallis was admitted to Madron Public Assistance Institute.

Bill Wallis remembered his great uncle as a bright, lively old man, if somewhat lonely. He enjoyed having a companion to talk to, and they discussed life in St Ives and Wallis would recount his experiences at sea. Bill Wallis saw nothing of the wild behaviour that others have written about - indeed, he felt offended by what he saw as unwarranted distortions of Alfred Wallis's character. Bill Wallis took meals to his great uncle; he related that on the Sabbath Wallis would cover his paintings with newspapers and spend the day reading a large family Bible.

After the publication of the correspondence following David Sylvester's article, Bill Wallis wrote a letter which was published in *The Times*. (Illustrated, right)

The discovery of Wallis's signature on ships' articles of agreement provides indisputable evidence of his seagoing experience, so Rowe's grandfather's statement can now be dismissed as nonsense. It is understood that there had previously been a serious falling out between Wallis and Albert Ward concerning the loss of some savings, so perhaps these remarks stemmed from bad feeling within the family. Additionally, there may have been an element of jealousy caused by the growing interest in Wallis's painting. Nevertheless, the unfortunate fact is that the doubts sown by Mr Rowe have influenced the perception of Wallis and his work.

In his compelling portrait of Alfred Wallis, *Alfred Wallis Cornish Primitive Painter*, 1967, Edwin Mullins discusses the question. Asking *'did he go to sea?'* He concludes:

*Personally I think it is most likely that he did go to sea, and that it does not matter much anyway.*

In an essay on Wallis, George Melly takes a similar stand:

*But as to whether Wallis ever went to sea there have been some doubts expressed. But perhaps it doesn't really matter anyway, given the confusion between reality and imagination in the mind of this genuine primitive.*

The confusion referred to above indicates the pernicious influence of Rowe's story, with its implication that Wallis was a fantasist.

---

**Wallis at sea**

Sir,—As a great nephew of the artist Alfred Wallis, I should like to comment on the discussion as to whether he ever went to sea. My father and I frequently visited Wallis at weekends and took him hot meals and a Sunday paper. These visits fascinated me: he would talk of sea voyages around the coasts of Cornwall and Newfoundland which I was firmly convinced he had made. Being such a religious person, I do not think he would have lied about this. Even then, as a boy, I admired his paintings, as the sea looked so realistic.

During my visits I would find him reading a very large black Bible. He was a deeply religious man; a little eccentric but certainly not mad.

**William Charles Wallis**
London SW18

It seems odd that there should be any doubt at all as to whether Wallis went to sea as so many of his paintings display an intimate knowledge of the subject. They contain a wealth of geographical and nautical know-how that could only have come from personal experience.

Is the question of Wallis's first-hand knowledge important? Yes, surely it matters a great deal. Wallis's life and experience are central to his work, as is the case with many creative people.

Wallis has been ill-served by a distorted myth and a desire to perpetuate the tale of the mad artist. For instance, a newspaper review of a play began:

*The stage is set in Alfred Wallis's living room where he rants and raves throughout the play.*

Artists, and certainly critics who wrote about art came, predominantly, from an educated, middle-class background; it may have been difficult for them to understand Wallis or the impenetrable world of the close-knit, working-class, harbour town that he inhabited. Yet surely the abundant visual evidence in his paintings belies the demeaning way he has been characterised. The very qualities we value in his work show a lively imagination, even humour. His paintings lift our spirits.

In the days of sail it was essential that seamen had their wits about them, and it was vital that each member of the crew could be relied upon to do their job properly. The owners of *Flying Scud* were very experienced seamen; Kelynack and Badcock would not have tolerated a crewman aboard who was not up to the mark. Joe Denley was a shrewd businessman, ship owner and merchant. He must have had confidence in Wallis's competence when he asked him to go to St Ives to set up a new business. Wallis and his wife were hardworking and well respected in the community and they earned enough from the business to buy their cottage in Back Road West.

Another oft-repeated, dismissive cliché that has become associated with Wallis is that he was semi-literate. Wallis wrote colloquially and would have spoken with a strong accent, and it is likely that his standard of literacy was comparable to that of his friends and neighbours in Downalong, St Ives. We should not let his erratic use of capital letters and misspelling obscure the fact that his letters convey a profound awareness of what he was doing and that his work differs from that of the other artists around him, whom he referred to as 'real artists'. He realised that they painted what they saw, whereas he painted what he knew.

His words have depth and meaning: *'I paint what used to be.'* He mourns the changes that have taken place, and knows that things will *'never be the same again'*, and that they have changed forever; the seine fishery is finished, the pilchards have disappeared. Ships no longer took barrels of Cornish pilchards to the Mediterranean. This and the associated sense of loss is the subject of his paintings. As Nicholson said, Wallis's intention was *'to inform a younger generation of how things were when he was young'*.

Bill Wallis collected newspaper clippings of reviews of Wallis's exhibitions. Amongst them was one by Leslie Geddes-Brown, the art critic of the *Daily Telegraph*, writing on 4th November 1992, where he begins with the usual dismissive:

*Alfred Wallis was a true paranoid, barely literate and, in later life, flea-ridden,* but goes on to state:
*Yet this old Cornish mariner was this century's greatest primitive painter. Without him the St Ives (modern) School of Artists would not have existed and the work of Ben Nicholson, Christopher Wood, Roger Hilton and Peter Lanyon could not have been the same.*

*This painted glass fishing float was presented as a genuine Wallis and was described on Hayle Gallery's website as 'a superb painted object, the most superb and tactile piece of work by Wallis we have ever seen' and priced £60,000.*

### Forgeries

Our view of Wallis has been distorted by the number of fakes and forgeries that have appeared on the market since 2008. The accessibility of the internet has furthered the deceitful practice of presenting forgeries as genuine. Many such images still appear online alongside genuine examples of Wallis's work. A significant number of forgeries were the subject of what became one of the largest cases ever brought by Cornwall Council and Trading Standards.

As the interest in Wallis's work has increased, the value of his paintings has risen greatly. Works originally bought from him for a few shillings or given to his friends during his lifetime now have considerable value. Meanwhile, art forgery and the marketing of fakes has become particularly prevalent in recent years. Unfortunate victims of this crime, many of whom have paid large sums of money for a painting, may not discover their mistake until they offer it for resale.

Since publishing the first edition of Alfred Wallis: Artist and Mariner, a number of individuals have sought my opinion on the authenticity of various paintings, and I have had some surprising and rewarding experiences as well as some amusing ones.

Two ladies brought me several childlike paintings they had bought at a car-boot sale, hoping I would confirm they were by Wallis. They were definitely not by Wallis, and when I said so, their dismayed reply was 'Who else can we ask?'

Another painting was brought to me by the owner who informed me that it had previously been rejected by an auctioneer. Showing three ships on the Fal, this painting was undoubtedly by Wallis, and on the back was an inscription by Jim Ede, making this an even more interesting find. (Painting illustrated on page 91).

In popular culture there is a view of the forger as a cunning rogue whose work is clever enough to fool the experts, but in reality this is simply defrauding people who have been deceived into putting their trust in the seller. I have come to hear of some distressing cases where buyers have parted with thousands of pounds for a forged painting they were led to believe was genuine; it is upsetting to hear from people who have been deceived in this way.

It seems futile to rely on the police to deal with art fraud. In the preceding years, the police seem to have gone to extraordinary lengths to avoid prosecuting a prolific forger in west Cornwall, despite the fact that in one investigation into his activities eight separate witnesses produced evidence against him. In this case neither the boards nor the paint in forgeries found in his possession matched materials the original artist regularly used. It was clear that the paintings had been copied from an illustrated catalogue of the artist's previously sold, original, paintings. The suspect remained under arrest for several months before the case was dropped; the forgeries were returned to him and found their way back onto the market.

*One of the paintings tested by Art Analysis and Research, and used in evidence by Cornwall Council/Trading Standards trial 2015. This fake still appears on the internet as genuine as do many of the fake pieces from the Hayle Gallery.*

*In a case brought by a private individual against a colleague of David Carter this painting was forensically tested at the University of Lincoln and found to have contained paint unavailable during Wallis's lifetime.*

*The two paintings (right) were featured in a television programme,* Hidden Paintings *(Televisionary). The programme commissioned Art Analysis and Research, London, who also carried out tests for Trading Standards, to perform a forensic test on paint samples. Findings showed that the paint used in these pictures was not available during Wallis's lifetime. Samples taken from genuine Wallis paintings contain lead, as did most paint in those days; no lead was present in the tested paintings.*

*The paintings illustrated were involved in the Television programme and the Cornwall Trading Standards case. While they share a recognisable artistic style, it is not that of Alfred Wallis. The ship in the painting, top right, has obviously been copied from the well-known Wallis painting in the Tate collection,* The Blue Ship.

Television programmes that trace the provenance of a work of art to determine its authenticity are currently popular. The viewer is interested to see if the painting is worth a fortune or a fake. In 2011, a west country television company invited me to participate in a similar show for the BBC that was to feature paintings by Wallis. I was asked to comment on twelve works sourced from a gallery in west Cornwall with a website that boasted an exclusive stock of Wallis originals. The programme featured a conservator explaining why she was convinced the paintings were genuine and I gave my reasons for believing they were not. Two of the paintings were to be sent to a specialist laboratory for forensic testing. Subsequently, analysis showed that paints used in all these pictures were available only after Wallis's death and, crucially, revealed the absence of lead, which was present in almost all paint until the 1950s. Despite this, the gallery owner ignored warnings from various sources, including other dealers, and continued to advertise for sale a large number fake Wallis items on the gallery's website. For example a glass fishing-float painted, perhaps, by someone with a maritime interest; it was of little value and could better be categorised as a piece of marine bric-a-brac, but on the website it was described as '*a superb painted object, the most superb and tactile piece of work by Wallis we have ever seen*' and the price was set at £60,000.

Gathering evidence against perpetrators of art fraud is a complex business and we should not underestimate the effort that Cornwall Trading Standards invested in preparing the case they brought to the Crown Court in 2015. It took several years to compile the evidence and it is to their credit that they were willing to take up the case.

Trading Standards were aware of Hayle Gallery's extraordinary dealings as they had received a number of complaints about it and they knew that the website was an elaborate scam designed to give credibility to an array of fakes by Wallis and artists such as Stanhope Forbes and John Brett.

After a painstaking investigation, Trading Standards had gathered enough information to bring the case to the Crown Court in June 2015. The gallery owner, David Carter, faced thirteen charges of fraud, and on the day of the trial he agreed to plead guilty to seven of them. He received a suspended jail sentence and a substantial fine. Proceedings revealed that he had purchased the paintings in question from such reliable sources of fine art as websites titled 'anyoldtat.com' and 'creditcrunchmyarse.com' for a few hundred pounds. We can only speculate as to where these paintings had originated or by whom they had been created.

Following the 1968 exhibition at the Penwith Galleries in St Ives and the Tate in London, curated by Sir Alan Bowness, interest in Wallis's work grew, and in the late 1960s and early 1970s it was well known that a man based in St Ives was faking Wallis paintings. The forgeries in the court case had clearly not been produced recently so it is possible that they had been created by this man.

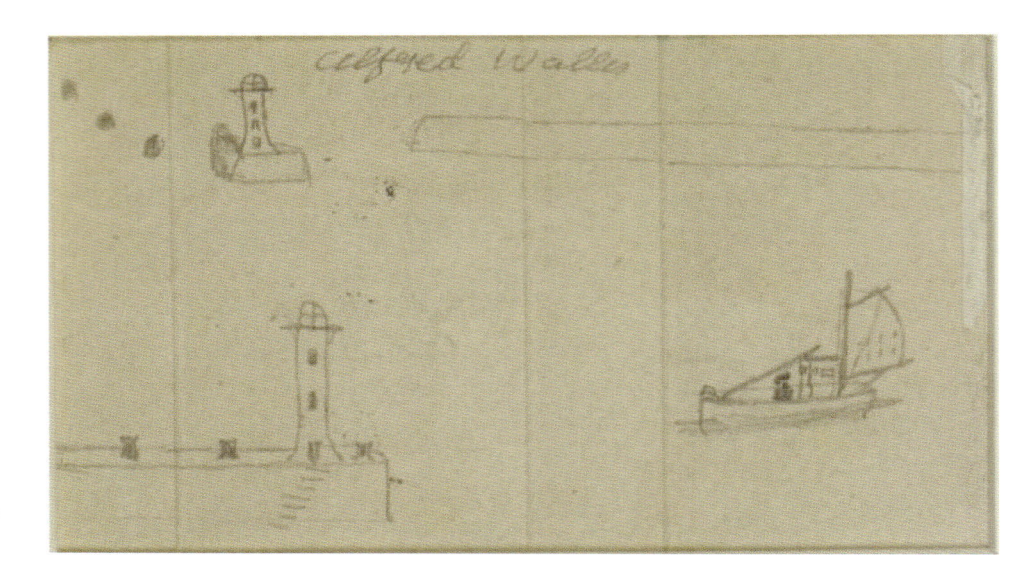

*The hesitant nature of this drawing and the uncharacteristic fishing boat made me doubt the authenticity of this piece. I asked a specialist to date the packet design. It was produced from the mid 1950s at least ten years after Wallis's death. Imperial Tobacco confirmed this date.*

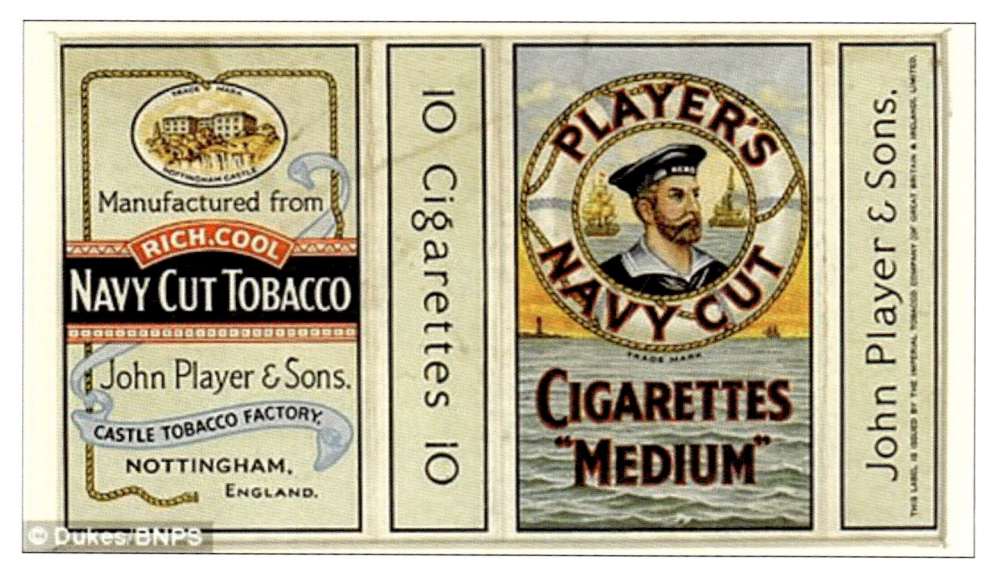

Another case of art fraud involving work purportedly by Wallis was brought to court by Dorset Trading Standards in 2016. In the spring of that year an art auctioneer from Duke's in Dorchester asked me to write a catalogue essay about a collection of Wallis items submitted to their forthcoming sale. The provenance sounded familiar. I heard that the pieces had come from a former fisherman who had grown up in St Ives and had inherited an old toolbox that contained several items by Wallis.

I realised that I knew this individual. I had initially been introduced to him in 2010, when the director of Penlee House Museum & Art Gallery invited me to look at some items that been brought in by a retired fisherman, which he thought had been drawn or painted by Alfred Wallis. He showed us some painted tin lids, some pencil drawings on cigarette packets and on an old magazine. He told us that the toolbox they had been stored in had fallen to pieces and had been thrown away. These items could have been classed as Wallis memorabilia, but were of interest nevertheless. Their tatty, scruffy nature suggested they were indeed made by Wallis, for what forger would go to the trouble of fabricating such 'slight' and comparatively low value items?

*This old fashioned blow-lamp was purported to have been painted and inscribed by Wallis - 'To Emma Perkin from Uncle Alfred'.*

In addition, the historical and geographical detail in the cigarette-packet drawings supported the likelihood that the items were genuine, and remarks in archive recordings indicating that Wallis had indeed made drawings on cigarette packets lent further plausibility to the former fisherman's story. Some of these cigarette packet drawings and tin-lids were later auctioned in Penzance, where they fetched unexpectedly high prices. However, in the following years it became apparent that this man's collection was expanding; a seemingly endless supply of dubious work was emerging and was being offered for sale at auction and at a local gallery.

I advised the auctioneer of my misgivings and refused to write an essay for their auction catalogue. A pre-auction exhibition of this consignment was held in the auction house's gallery, and the collection, valued at an estimated £125,000, was featured in the national press. At the request of the director of the Auction House I went to Dorchester to see the exhibition. It confirmed what I already knew; that I had seen some of the items several months previously when another art auctioneer showed them to me and I had expressed doubts about their authenticity. On my advice, he did not accept any of these items for his auction.

A wooden chest with a ship painted on the inside of the lid was said to have contained the entire collection. A painting of a schooner in silhouette entitled '*Schooner in St Ives Bay*', was featured in the collection, yet laughably this large painting could not have fitted into the chest. Amongst the smaller items on display was a rather hesitant depiction of a motor fishing boat sketched on the back of a Player's cigarette packet. Although motor powered fishing boats were present in St Ives during Wallis's latter years there, I had not seen a depiction of such vessels in his work. His paintings of fishing boats describe his own experiences working under sail.

An online press report showed this drawing together with the front of the cigarette packet with its distinctive Player's design showing the sailor and the lifebelt. An image was sent to a specialist historian and to Imperial Tobacco to be dated and both confirmed that this particular design had only been in circulation from the mid-1950s - more than ten years after Wallis's death. Clearly a forger had taken the trouble to obtain old cigarette packets to further the deception but had failed to realise that the design had subtly changed over time. This seems to demonstrate a curious criminal trait - a mixture of devious cunning and utter stupidity.

I informed the auctioneer of these findings, but they did not respond. However, Dorset Trading Standards intervened, seizing the entire collection on the day before the auction. Subsequently they initiated forensic paint analysis, which found that all the painted items in the collection had been made with paint unavailable during Wallis's lifetime. On 30th October 2016 Duke's pleaded guilty to eight charges under unfair trading regulations and were ordered to pay fines and costs.

It is hard to accept that the fraudsters behind this scam have not been pursued by the authorities. They are undeterred and appear to be still active. Even though the authenticity of every piece in this collection had been thoroughly discredited Dorset Trading Standards returned all of these items to the vendor.

*Too large to fit into the wooden box in which it was supposed to have been found, this fake Wallis painting of a schooner had been painted on plywood taken from an old tea chest. Similarities in the depiction of the quay and lighthouse in this piece to those in the cigarette packet drawing on page 232 suggest they could have been made by the same hand. The court heard that the items in the collection 'were produced with deceptive intent, in relatively recent times in order to resemble authentic pieces by Wallis.'*

*The box with the painted lid and furnished with old newspapers was said to have contained the whole collection. On the day before it was due to be auctioned, Dorset Trading Standards seized the consignment. Later, forensic analysis showed all the painted items to be fake.*

# Appendix II
## Recorded memories
People who knew Alfred Wallis

**Dr Roger Slack's recorded memories of Alfred Wallis**

Dr Slack came to St Ives as a GP in 1947 after serving as a naval surgeon aboard destroyers in the North Atlantic in the Second World War. Many of the artists in the town became his patients, as did St Ives people who had known Alfred Wallis, his friends, neighbours and relations. Dr Slack realised the importance of preserving their memories, and recorded conversations with them about their recollections of Wallis. These interviews add another dimension to the story and give an insight as to how Wallis and his paintings were regarded by those around him. They almost form a biography in themselves.

**Painted jug**
Oil on painted earthenware 13¼ in (33.6 cm) high
Private Collection

### Nancy Ward

*'He did go to sea. And he's been in my mother's house and telling my grandfather all about his experiences, he was a little cabin boy in one of the big boats. I suppose in them days it was the three mast ships. And he told him that he wasn't more than between 9 and 10 that he was in the Bay of Biscay. So what d'you call that? That isn't only land is it?'*

### George Farrell

*'He finished the sea, I've heard him say he went to sea as a galley boy at nine, out in Newfoundland. See they had to work in they day.'*

### Thomas Curnow

*'Proper old type of fisherman. ... But he was a boy to sea. He went to Ireland somewhere on the fishing boats from Newlyn and that's where he was, in Penzance, before he came here ... but if ever he had anything it was a jersey, and never see him with other than his blue jersey on. No coats or nothing. Old, tough old bloke I think. Very healthy.'*

### Thomas Curnow

*'Always had a blue jersey on. Never saw him dressed up with collar and tie. Very small fellow, very active and quick. Was a boy to sea in fishing boats from Newlyn. Went to Ireland. Never saw him in other than blue jersey even in winter. No coat - tough old chap.'*

### Nancy Ward

*'Well anyway she married him and for all I saw they were very happy and comfortable. And they were just one "highth". Well you wouldn't ... to look at he and to look at Granny you would think they were one age. ... She was years older than he but I said "Don't matter for that. Did they get on alright?" "Yes" she said, "They were alright; Alfred's alright, but he's a boy to she."'*

### Thomas Lander

*'He had his Marine Stores down on the Wharf down close to Robin Nance's shop; the store was a kind of cellar, he lived over.'*

Wallis's first business was situated next to the Salvation Army Citadel but later moved to Bethesda Hill. At first the neighbours were apprehensive about Marine Stores, but on meeting Wallis Nancy Ward's grandfather Sam Green ...

### Nancy Ward

'"Oh!" he said. "I like that little chap and I'm going to have him in for bit of company in the evenings" and he did, he used to come in and they got on splendid.'

### George Farrell

'I believe he did very well at it too. He used to buy 'most anything, you know, buying and selling.'

### Nancy Ward

'He used to ... go away in different parts of the town and buy hard junk such as pieces of chain and old bedsteads and bring it home; and fishermen, if they had a length of old chain which was finished for their use, they used to drag it up in front of his shop and strike a bargain.'

### Thomas Lander

'Course, he used to buy any kind of metal, Iron or rags and bones. ... As boys we weren't very well off for Saturday spending money and we used to go on the beaches and collect small quantities of rags and bones, there of four of us; but they had to be clean and he wouldn't have old bones with meat on them. Then we used to take them up there and he would take a look at them and probably might say "tuppence". We would probably think them worth a ha'penny more and try to drive a bargain, but if Mr Wallis said tuppence, it was tuppence'.

### Jacob Ward

'Used to go once a fortnight about, all depends on what stuff is coming in, or maybe once a month and he had that little cart he had in them days, loaded, and we used to go into this big yard and take all the stuff off[... I was always hurrying him on so as we could go to dinner see. I've been there dozens of times.'

### Mrs Curnow

'Used to wear a bowler hat; well, I never saw him without.'

Jessie Farrell

*'And then he lent a lot of money to fishermen, to Captains of boats, but you mustn't say anything outside.'*

George Farrell

*'… talk about Grandad Wallis when he used to, once upon a time he made ice-cream. Somebody brought this recipe for this ice-cream … I think someone trading to Italy on a ship brought the recipe home and he used to make it. He had an ice-cream barrow … push it sometimes to Penzance to sell ice-cream.'*

Nancy Ward

*'He had a little donkey, shay. Sunday afternoons in the spring he would go and make ice cream; mind, he was clean, you could eat from him.'*

Jessie Farrell

*'Yes my father went up to Scarborough at the time, and he said, "If you get any nice recipes for ice cream, bring 'em home, and we'll make 'em." My granny used to make them, and he used to sell them, over Hayle for the regatta and everything. He was a good businessman.'*

Joe Burrell

*'He used to stand at the market house with two or three others on Saturday night, in the summer. Ha'penny a sandwich, and they reckoned he got a pound or thirty shillings a night - course if it rained it was a washout for them, and school treats.'*

Thomas Lander

*'He was quiet man and an industrious man, he could do lots of things apart from that. He had, during the summer time, a little ice-cream business, which he used to make ice-cream in the afternoon and about four o'clock in the afternoon … he had a little barrow … and pop, he used to put there, too, in it and he wheeled it all over the Wharf to the Market Place.'*
(RJ: He also made and sold sandwiches and pop)

### Thomas Lander

*'Along with the pop he would make ha'penny windmills; a little bit of stick with a pin on top, four pieces of wood and a little bit of square wallpaper they used to cut up and paste on so the wind would take it and revolve it around. That was his plan of a windmill. Ha'penny and a penny each.'*

### Nancy Ward

*'Now there was two very loose character boys here. ... Two outcast boys if you will and they'd do anything for - I don't know that they drank, I never heard that they did - and they went out and they took some lead, some brass from the wreck. They had no business to do it you know, and they came to Granda Wallis, of course he being in the Marine Store he bought it from them. They said they hadn't touched it from the wreck, they found it on the beach. He innocently bought it from them. When it was found out of course it was trouble for Grandad. ... And poor old Granda was took up. He was in jail all over one night at the police station. Everybody was up in arms and all the neighbours and everybody was all upset.'*

### Emily Woolcock

*'But granny was a very very kind woman ... I've never heard her grumble, and they always had plenty of everything. They must have done very well.'*

### George Farrell

*'Oh I know he tried various things. I don't think he made a flop at very much you know. I think he'd lose interest in one particular thing and go and try something else.'*

### Thomas Curnow

*'He made good in the old iron. He wasn't bad when he finished but poor old chap was a long time that he lived on what he did save. Very careful, didn't drink or anything; not a man that would waste anything.'*

### Emily Woolcock

*Dr R. Slack: 'So he started (to paint) before she died?'*
*Emily Woolcock: 'Oh yes. He was always scribbling on little bits of cardboard. Yes he always had little pieces of cardboard. But then we didn't used to take any notice of it. ... We used to laugh at it really. Mother used to say, "That's like a child's picture, all boats, mind, nothing but boats."'*

### George Farrell

'silly really you know, 'cause I could have got different paintings of his, but used to laugh at them, we did as children. He used to do quite a bit of sketching when he had the Marine Stores, that's lots of years ago when I was eight years old.'

### Sara Langford

'He came here from Penzance. You could tell she wasn't a local person. She had a different dialect altogether from this part of the world. But she was a Salvationist.'

### Jacob Ward

'and he had his bowler hat on, and a great jersey he had on ... No, he was a marvellous little chap, little short chap. Always had a watery eye ... He was a very sprightly man, he was small but he was very quick.'

### George Farrell

'He used to wear heavy gauge sort of navy blue trousers and a fisherman's jersey. He used to go along, very small fellow.'

### Jessie Farrell

'...and there's one great disappointment to him and he used to nearly cry. She had three children by Alfred Wallis and neither one of them lived any length of time. She had three and they died. He was very disappointed.'

### Nancy Ward

'He used to play like that but he could do a very good job, you know, for him in that way. I never heard him sing, but Mrs Wallis she was a beautiful singer.'

### Emily Woolcock

'Well, I remember him as a little girl. Used to go out there practically nearly every day see. 'Course they were elderly then. Well he was a little short man with a moustache. He was always very kind to me. They used to say "Oh he was a grump of a man" but I couldn't say it ... '

### Nancy Ward

*'This was after Grandma died, and he never slept upstairs no more after she died. He used to sleep with a little box or something in front of the window so I've heard them say. I never went there in the night.'*

### Emily Woolcock

*'I can see Grampa Wallis on top of the stairs now Lord Baden-Powell on the wall there. Queen Victoria somewhere else. And over here was Peter walking over the sea. And they did have marvellous china … marvellous.'*

### Joe Burrell

*'Course, Mrs Wallis was a dear old soul you know, but I don't think he … when she died … I think he finished going upstairs. He was telling me "The devil's up the chimney in our place".'*

### Thomas Lander

*'he started little bits of sketches of boats and vessels and steamboats and landscapes and some was drawed on bits of cardboard, and some on covers of tins, anything you know.'*

**Painted box**
Oil on wood 6 x 11½ x 6 in (15 x 29 x 15 cm) Private Collection

George Farrell

'He used to have a passion for painting mackerel boats, you know, mackerel luggers, double-end mackerel luggers, and they used to be used to make a frieze of them all along the wainscotting. ... He used to paint on everything, he used to paint on the cups as well, nothing was safe from where paint could go, like. I suppose he was a character really. Mind, I think as, if you look closely at what he painted, for instance a mackerel lugger, and the sails and the boat itself, the detail in it was true. ... But I believe his paintings again are quite valuable, but you could have had them for taking away. He had so many of them that I don't suppose he knew what to do with them. I suppose a lot of them got burned or chucked away. ... I've seen schooners that he's done, and when you look back, although some of the detail of it is out of proportion and so on, it is accurate. The rigging is a hundred per cent really, like your foot ropes and things like that are out of proportion. Though I suppose that some of your shrouds and ratlines on some of the paintings he done were very big, but I suppose that he thought that your neck was resting on it when you were in the rigging, so he made it that big.'

Thomas Lander

'And he used to explain to them in his way the detail of every part of the sail and what it was used for. Whether he was any part connected with the sea before he came here I don't know, but he had that part about him that he knew what the sail was for, and the ropes.'

Joe Burrell

'And he wouldn't have any paint, only the yacht paint, called it yacht paint for the boats, see, he would only buy cheap little camel hair brushes, you know, you can't press on them or anything, can you? He said, "I don't use the paints artists use, mine's the real paint. Don't want the muck they've got."'

**Emily Woolcock**

*' ... when my Granny died, I mean I am going now when my Granny died one week my Mother used to make dinner for him and then my Aunt Jess used to make dinner for him another week ... and every time I practically went in he used to say "'ere you are my cheel carry this 'ome", well it was like a stone jar like we used to get the marmalade in those days, was stone jars; but they were all boats and all, painted around this. Well, I used to carry them home. Mother used to say to me "Well don't for heaven's sake Emily bring any more of them in because ... throw them in the dustbin." ... He used to draw with the mind of a child. Boats by galore, and my mother used to be here washing 'em off with soda. Yes the stone jars, I've had scores of them, see, if only I had one today.'*

*Dr R. Slack: 'I've got one.'*
*Emily Woolcock: 'Have you? Well that'll show you, that'll show that I'm telling the truth see. There you are, see, scores I've had, and mother said, well she used to say a few words, "Put them in the dustbin, I don't want no more of them brought in here." Only he thought he was doing something see. Never gave us any money or anything like that. Never passed any money. But you could have a jar, or a piece of cardboard with a boat on it see.'*

**Nancy Ward**

*'So he said to Father one day, "Jacob", he said, "I wonder what they artist fellows can think of these here, and my bits of cardboards." He said, "They must think something by them Alfred", he said, "to buy them". "So when there was a show day on I pinned up two or three of my little ships", he said, "To the door", and in walked two gentlemen, and they said, "Are you showing pictures?" He said, "If you've a mind to call them pictures." So he looked at them and he said, "Are you selling them?" and he said, "I'll give 'em to 'ee, I don't want to sell they, I'll give 'em to 'ee." So he said, "Oh no, I can't expect you to do that." Well any rate, after a while they sent and said to him, "Will you paint two pictures like the small ones we had from you?" and they sent off fifteen shillings.'*

### George Farrell

*'He used to be forever painting. He used to have - oh - he used to paint on the table and on the wall, paint on anything that you gave him. Funny thing, everybody used to think that he was eccentric you know, but nobody took much interest in his paintings. For instance, you could look around at a lot of artists that have painted nearer the thing than you thought he did. You know as a child. His paintings always seemed to resemble what you yourself would do as a child. Just before the war, when the Alba went ashore, I remember him painting a picture of the Alba. But he brought the lighthouse in as well as the Alba, and the wreck of the lifeboat. Now the lifeboat was on the Island side, and so was the Alba, but it was impossible to see the lighthouse from there, and that's what always stuck in my memory.'*

### Emily Ward

*'He was having a pension then. He said "Take my fortnight's pension, carry 'un up and give [Thomas] Curnow up there towards the widows of the lifeboat disaster."'*
(RJ - at the time of the loss of the *John and Eliza Stych* lifeboat)

**Painted bellows**
Oil on wood 26 x 13 x 27½ in (66 x 33 x 70 cm)
Private Collection

### George Farrell

'… ever since I can remember painting on everything and you could have had the paintings for nothing. He painted on cardboard, anything he could get hold of. I suppose he was a character in his way, I think all the people were characters in those days. … but granny always used to say "Take this out to Grandad" or either myself or one of my brothers go and off we used to trot with his dinner Saturday. But he was a queer old boy.'

### Thomas Lander

'Though sometimes they were not very eyeable to look at you know, he had the idea of what they was wanted for, and he would explain to those visitors you know, and tell them all about it. … So he used to explain his work to anyone who really wanted to know but he never used to think, once he found out you were trying to take the mickey out of him, or a ride, you could never have no more to do with Alfred.'

### Mrs Cothey

'Oh yes, after his wife died. You'd hear someone say "Everything in Mr Wallis's is nothing but boats, he's painted up everything". He did too. … o'course we've known since he was the cleverest artist around. He would have a tin of paint and a paintbrush and he'd go for it.'

### Jessie Farrell

'Mother used to cook for the old man. What he used to like most of all was herrings stewed in onions. … and Willie used to carry his dinner every day and when we used to leave the plates there, and little basins with his dinner, he used to draw on them and paint. My Mother didn't know they was any good, she used to wash them off, it took a lot to wash them off. … That's where modern art came from, isn't it. He used to draw with the mind of a child, boats by galore and my Mother used to be there washing 'em off with soda.'

### George Farrell

'As a youngster, I should think I could paint better myself! But I believe his paintings again are quite valuable but you could have had them for taking away. He had so many of them that I don't suppose he knew what to do with them. I suppose a lot of them got burned or chucked away. … he was quite a character; he used to smoke, he'd smoke a pipe. Black twist! Fly killer. He smoked from the time I remembered him, I suppose cherry wood pipe.'

### Thomas Curnow
'The artises must have seen something about him. And then there's a book about him. I've never seen it.'

### Sarah Langford
'He said the Devil was upstairs. He never went up there. He made up a little bed in behind the table because he was a very small man, oh! very small. ... And he used to take long walks, nothing new for him to walk to Penzance and back. Very long walks. He was a very active little fellow you know. Oh he was very springy on his legs, springy.'

### Nancy Ward
'He did go funny, he did. Well he said ... I used to say "Granda why don't you come up and live with we? You've got the little room, that'll be your room and don't worry you'll have lots of company up with we." "No I aren't going to give up my own house to live with nobody." ... "No", he said, "I am going to stop here while I live, while I can." Well then he got off his head you see. Went awfully queer.'

### Mrs Cothey
'She could see things, and he could hear. He could hear the Devil, the Devil was always upstairs. "Oh my dear", she used to say, "He is going mad, all he do think about is the Devil."'

### Joe Burrell
''Cause I remember when Mr Ben Nicholson went into Madron Union to see him, he came out next day. He said "there's an old chap in there, he's nothing to employ his mind and he's told me to bring in, to get some paint and brushes for him, buy these in Burrell's shop I have all my paint in there. What sort of paint does he have?" I pointed out the paint he do have, tins of paint, pound tins there. None of the small stuff, and the brushes. Nicholson bought some and took 'em in to him.'

### Jacob Ward
'but he was a wonderful old man in his time. I can't see nothing missing from grandfather Wallis. But I do know, he's dead and gone; I do go up to the cemetery and look at his grave there, and I said "Poor old chap, he's sure tombed down he is." Some tomb he has up there hasn't he? Cor grief, who put that up there? Did the artists?'

### Margaret Mellis

'Only a few artists appreciated Wallis's work when he was alive. It has taken about 40 years for the general public to see their originality, beauty and total unadulterated truth. It is because of these qualities that other artists are so influenced by him.' [36]

Transcripts of conversations with Edwin Mullins. From *Memories of Alfred Wallis*, Dr Roger Slack.

### Barbara Hepworth

'Ben took me several times to see him. He was incredibly small and I think his eyes must have been grey-green. They were very serious eyes but he had a twist to his mouth which denoted a high sense of humour, and he wore a cap and an apron covered in paint. ... and he was the most serious and dignified person I've ever met ... I never, of course saw him in anger.'

### Bernard Leach

'His paintings on exhibition now are to me experiences. They are his experiences put down without rules, without professional paints, painted on a flat table so that everything, like handwriting goes off into the top right-hand corner of the rectangle. ... it was the creative man. He blossomed as a flower on a blackthorn in spring.'

### Patrick Heron

'Wallis is the most amazing case of a completely innocent mind pictorially speaking grappling with an intensity and passionate understanding with his surroundings, and with the surroundings which were the reality not only for himself but for his community. ... There are technical ways in which Wallis's influence on Wood and Nicholson, and later on Peter Lanyon can be measured. In colours, for instance, a sort of dirty white, a very pale cerulean blue, pale grey and a very dark pleasantly essential St Ives green, the green of the headlands and salty grass; these persisted right through into Lanyon's own paintings for instance, and in the case of Christopher Wood, ditto.

### Edwin Mullins

'I was astonished by the variety of mood, of technique, of colour, of form in what a lot of people think of as a man who just painted one boat after the other time after time.'

### Patrick Heron

'One could in fact list technical innovations, for instance drawing in wet white paint with a 6B pencil producing a line dug into the paint. This is a thing that didn't occur to Picasso but it is something that Nicholson took over from Wallis quite instinctively. ... but hit upon formal ways of expressing himself, which had the utmost relevance to twentieth century masters. But I think that the magic about Wallis is the complete identity between the image and the reality.'

### Alan Bowness

'One too often got the image of Wallis as one little ship on a little bit of card, and some of these are beautiful. But there's more to it. In the catalogue introduction I've allowed myself a certain hint of Paradise Lost and paradise that one hopes will be gained in heaven as it were. I do think this is strong in Wallis ... because it does seem to me that he is one of the major figures in twentieth century, on a par with, say, Sickert or Matthew Smith. Now if you regard him as a primitive painter, this tends to be dismissive, and one doesn't really appreciate the quality of his work. ... They appear in the history of painting at a moment when things get a little too precious, over sophisticated, too technical perhaps, and suddenly you have someone with all the natural gifts ... which seem to have come from nowhere. Here you have this man with an intense personal vision that seems to force everybody to rethink what they are doing. I can't help thinking of Wallis as a medieval or early renaissance artist. ... It's partly the fact that he wasn't concerned with perspective, that he uses proportion to indicate the importance of things ... this whole intensity of vision.

### Barbara Hepworth

'In August 1942 we heard that he had died. By the good offices of Adrian Stokes who worked so hard for three days, we achieved, instead of a pauper's grave, a private grave. Many of us stood there watching the tiny coffin lowered with, I must say, tears in our eyes. But also a certain happiness that it had been the way he really wanted it. Every time I saw him he said, "These are for you to copy off" He knew his experience of walking around the harbour, going under a bridge, seeing the boats come in, was true information which what he called "real artists" could take off from, as he said. But of course he certainly didn't know how much we all learned and took off from him. By this magical sense of reality of colour and tone, which he did so simply and so truthfully and which inspired us all.'

# Endnotes

Page

| | | |
|---|---|---|
| 8 | 1 | *Alfred Wallis, Cornish Primitive Painter.* Edwin Mullins, Macdonald, London, 1967. |
| | 2 | Alfred Wallis. Letter to J. Ede. 6th April 1935. |
| 11 | 3 | *The old man of the seapiece.* David Sylvester, *Sunday Times*, 31st January 1965. |
| 14 | 4 | *Alfred Wallis and His Family: Fact and Fiction.* Peter Barnes, St Ives Trust Archive Study Centre, 1997. |
| 25 | 5 | *Alfred Wallis, Primitive.* Sven Berlin, Nicholson & Watson, 1949. |
| 32 | 6 | Agreement and Account of Crew No. 420. Peter Barnes, Cornish Records Office. |
| 36 | 7 | *Alfred Wallis, Primitive.* Sven Berlin, Nicholson & Watson, 1949. |
| | 8 | *The Merchant Schooners.* Volume 1, page 102, Basil Greenhill. |
| 47 | 9 | *The Merchant Schooners.* Volume 1. Basil Greenhill. |
| 74 | 10 | Tony Pawlyn, Head of Research at the Bartlett Maritime Research Centre and Library, National Maritime Museum Cornwall. |
| 88 | 11 | The owner of this painting brought it to me in January 2009. He inherited it from his aunt who had been given the painting by her neighbour in Mullion, the artist Gwinneth Jones-Parry, whom she had looked after in her old age. Gwinneth Jones-Parry was the widow of the Hungarian artist and author István Szegedi-Szuts (1892-1959) who came to Britain in 1936. His books include My War and Letters from Stalingrad. He showed work at the Redfern Gallery in London, and also at Newlyn Art Gallery. A self-portrait by him is in the collection of Falmouth Art Gallery. Jim Ede had given the painting *Three Sailing Vessels on a River* to István(Stevan) and Gwinneth on their marriage. The inscription on the back of this painting reads: 'To Stevan and Gwinneth their marriage 1937 from Jim Ede painting by Alfred Wallis'. The back of the painting has never been disturbed. The late Michael Harrison, then director of Kettle's Yard, remarked that it was in a 'typical Jim Ede frame'. |
| 90 | 12 | Penzance Shipping Registers, Cornwall Record Office (Ref: - CRO: MSR/PENZ/3) and the Penzance Sea Fishing Boat Registers, Cornwall Record Office (Ref: - CRO: MSR/PENZ/5). Secondary sources - contemporary newspaper files - Morrab Library & Cornwall Studies Centre, Redruth. Thanks to Tony Pawlyn Head of Research, Bartlett Maritime Research Centre and Library, National Maritime Museum Cornwall. March 2012. |
| 101 | 13 | *Fishing in Cornwall, Past and Present.* John McWilliams. Unpublished mss. |
| 116 | 14 | *Alfred Wallis, Primitive.* Sven Berlin, Nicholson & Watson, 1949. |
| 120 | 15 | *Alfred Wallis, Primitive.* Sven Berlin, Nicholson & Watson, 1949. |
| 134 | 16 | *Alfred Wallis, Primitive.* Sven Berlin (quoting Mr Armour), Nicholson & Watson, 1949. |
| 144 | 17 | *Horizon Magazine.* Article by Ben Nicholson, Volume VII, No 37, 1943. |
| | 18 | *Oxford Times.* Ben Nicholson. |
| | 19 | *Alfred Wallis, Primitive.* Sven Berlin, Nicholson & Watson, 1949. |
| | 20 | *Horizon Magazine.* Article by Ben Nicholson, Volume VII, No 37, 1943. |
| 146 | 21 | *Alfred Wallis, Primitive.* Sven Berlin, Nicholson & Watson, 1949. |
| 151 | 22 | Christopher Wood letter to Ben Nicholson, from St Ives, Autumn 1928 (WNA) From *Art and Life: Ben Nicholson, Winifred Nicholson, Christopher Wood, Alfred Wallis, William Staite Murray, 1920-1931*, Jovan Nicholson, page 136. |
| | 23 | From *Art and Life: Ben Nicholson, Winifred Nicholson, Christopher Wood, Alfred Wallis, William Staite Murray, 1920-1931*, Jovan Nicholson, page 136. |
| 152 | 24 | As 23. |
| 153 | 25 | *Ben Nicholson*, David Baxandall, Methuen, London, 1962. |
| 154 | 26 | *The Merchant Schooners.* Volume 1. Basil Greenhill. |
| 156 | 27 | *The Modern, The Primitive and the Picturesque.* Charles Harrison, Scottish Arts Council, 1987. |
| | 28 | *The Poetry of What Used To Be.* Edwin Mullins, *Studio International*; Autumn Book Supplement, November 1966. |
| 186 | 29 | Sven Berlin writing in Horizon Magazine 1943. |
| 200 | 30 | *The Merchant Schooners.* Volume II, page 24. Basil Greenhill. |
| 210 | 31 | *Fishing in Cornwall, Past and Present.* John McWilliams and Eddie Murt. Unpublished mss. |
| | 32 | Wallis's letter to Jim Ede April 1935. |
| 216 | 33 | Sven Berlin writing in *Horizon* Magazine 1943. |
| | 34 | Conversation between Edwin Mullins and Alethea Garstin. |
| 228 | 35 | *Wallis & The Sea Images of the Sea.* Catalogue essay, Bede Gallery, Tyne and Wear, 1996. |
| 254 | 36 | *Wallis & The Sea Images of the Sea.* Catalogue essay, Bede Gallery, Tyne and Wear, 1996. |